# Commentary
## on
## Insurance
## Law

## COIL
### Volume 1 No. 4
### © 01/01/2019

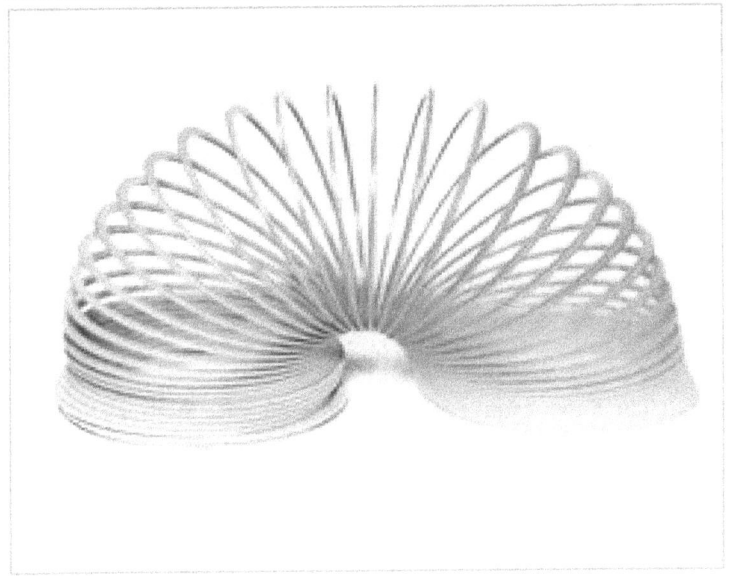

# TABLE OF CONTENTS

## Appraisal

Whenever a first party property claim reaches an impasse and the insured and the insurer cannot agree on the amount of loss the standard fire insurance policy provides a alternative dispute solution to determine the amount of loss called appraisal.

Appraisal is a type of arbitration that exists in every first party property insurance policy. It exists to establish the amount of loss when there is a dispute between the insured and the insurer as to the amount of loss. The appraisers' duty is limited to the damages and the appraisers have no right to discuss or rule on coverage issues.

The basic agreement provides:

> If we and you disagree on the value of the property or the amount of loss, either may make written demand for an appraisal of the loss. In this event, each party will select a competent and impartial appraiser. The two appraisers will select an umpire. If they cannot agree, either may request that selection be made by a judge of a court having jurisdiction. The appraisers will state separately the value of the property and amount of loss. If they fail to agree, they will submit their differences to the umpire. A decision agreed to by any two will be binding. Each party will:
>
> **a.** Pay its chosen appraiser; and
>
> **b.** Bear the other expenses of the appraisal and umpire equally.
>
> If there is an appraisal, we will still retain our right to deny the claim.

This condition sets up the rules that the insurer, insured and appraisers must follow.

Almost all property insurance policies contain an "appraisal" clause similar to that in the Standard Fire Insurance Policy that provides:

> In case the insured and this company shall fail to agree as to the actual cash value or the amount of loss, then, on the written demand of either, each shall select a competent and disinterested appraiser and notify the other of the appraiser selected within 20 days of such demand. The appraisers shall first select a competent and disinterested umpire; and failing for 15 days to agree upon such umpire, then, on request of the insured or this company, such umpire shall be selected by a judge of a court of record in the state in which the property covered is located. The appraisers shall then appraise the loss, stating separately actual cash value and loss to each item; and failing to agree, shall submit their differences, only, to the umpire. An award in writing, so itemized, of any two when filed with this company shall determine the amount of actual cash value and loss. Each appraiser shall be paid by the party selecting him and the expenses of appraisal and umpire shall be paid by the parties equally. (Standard Fire Policy)

In some states appraisal is not considered to be an arbitration, but is still enforceable and can be made a judgment by a court of competent jurisdiction.

The submission to the appraisers should be in writing, instructing that the parties do not want the appraisers to follow hard and fast, arbitrary, or fictitious rules in determining actual cash value, but to consider all evidence presented to them so that their award will serve to fully indemnify or compensate the insured for the actual loss he or she has sustained and at the same time not place him or her in a better position than he or she was in just before the fire.

By the appraisal provision, the insured and the company promise that if they cannot agree as to the amount of loss and claim they can submit their differences to a panel of three impartial arbitrators, called "appraisers." The decision of the appraisers regarding the amount of loss is binding on both parties. Appraisal should be used as a last resort when all efforts to reach an agreed amount of loss with the insured have failed. The appraisal provision is optional, and neither the insured nor the insurer is obligated to invoke that provision.

Under civil practice rules, appraisal can be a formal proceeding at which witnesses are subpoenaed to testify; evidence, both oral and documentary, can be produced to the arbitrators; and, within the limited scope of the appraisal, a trial, much like that in a lawsuit, can be had.

The activities of the appraisers are limited to decide the amount of loss and the value of the property in question. (*Jefferson Insurance Company of New York v. Superior Court*, 3 Cal. 3d 398, 90 Cal. Rptr. 608 (1970).) The appraisers cannot make decisions outside the limited scope of the policy language. They cannot find that the insured did not own the property, that the insured had no interest in it, that the insured was not entitled to recovery under policy exclusions, that the insured presented a fraudulent claim, or that the loss exceeds the policy limits.

In *Kirkwood v. California State Automobile Association Inter-Insurance Bureau*, 193 Cal.App.4th 49, 122 Cal.Rptr 3d 480, No. A128131 (Cal.App. Dist.1 02/28/2011), the California Court of Appeal refused to allow an insurer to compel appraisal until the declaratory relief action filed by the insured to determine the proper method of calculation of the actual cash value loss was first determined. The insured claimed it should be based on the condition of the property while the insurer argued that it should be determined by replacement cost less physical depreciation calculated only on the age of the item.

Douglas Kirkwood asserted that the California State Automobile Association Inter-Insurance Bureau (CSAA) improperly interpreted and applied the 2004 amendments to California Insurance Code Section 2051, which set out the precise method of determining actual cash value of lost or injured property under an open policy of fire insurance. CSAA asked the trial court to compel appraisal. The trial court denied, *without prejudice*, CSAA's motion to compel appraisal, reasoning that Kirkwood had properly invoked its declaratory relief powers to resolve a matter that was outside the scope of a statutory and contractual appraisal.

Kirkwood was insured by CSAA under a homeowner's policy. It was an "open" policy in which the value of the covered items was not agreed upon but was left to be determined following a loss. The policy provided that CSAA would pay actual cash value or the replacement cost of lost or damaged personal property. He submitted his personal property claim to CSAA, setting forth a physical depreciation amount based on the actual condition of each item at the time of the loss. CSAA provided Kirkwood with a contents inventory summary, which showed that a blanket depreciation schedule was applied to certain categories of property. For instance, many items were depreciated at 50 to 80 percent, and the depreciation was tied to the age of the item without regard to its condition.

## Appraisals Can be Waived

The right to appraisal can be waived. Although there is no single test for waiver of the right to compel arbitration, waiver may be found where the party seeking arbitration has:

- previously taken steps inconsistent with an intent to invoke arbitration;

- unreasonably delayed in seeking arbitration; or

- acted in bad faith or with willful misconduct.

At a minimum, the failure to plead arbitration as an affirmative defense is an act inconsistent with the later assertion of the right to arbitrate.

In *W. P. Sevier, Et Al v. United States Fidelity & Guaranty*, 497 So. 2d 1380 (1986), the Louisiana Supreme Court, Appellate Panel dealt with a case where after receiving a reconstruction estimate for $89,569.59, the adjuster asked for a second bid which was for $59,000. The adjuster forwarded a copy of the second bid to plaintiffs' attorney. Thereafter, the plaintiffs' attorney demanded the amount of the original estimate in settlement of the claim. One month later, he sent a bid of $88,716 from a third contractor. The adjuster notified the plaintiffs' attorney that USF&G demanded an appraisal. The plaintiffs refused to participate in the appraisal procedure, demanded settlement of the claim, and filed a lawsuit. The court concluded:

We conclude that the demand for appraisal by USF&G was not made within sixty days of receipt of a satisfactory proof of loss, and that plaintiff was therefore not required to submit to the demanded appraisal procedure. Thus, his lawsuit was not premature. Consequently, the exception of prematurity was properly dismissed by the trial court. Because of this finding, we do not reach the issue of whether the appraisal clause violates the provisions of La. Rev. Stat. Ann. 22:629(2).

It is incumbent on every insurer and insured to elect the right to appraisal promptly or risk losing it altogether. It is usually best to tender the amount the insurer believes it owes and advise the insured that, if the insured disputes the decision of the insurer, the insured has the right to demand appraisal. In the event that there is an appraisal and the appraisers find the amount of loss is more than the amount paid the insurer will pay the difference. If, on the other hand, the appraisers find less than the amount advanced, the insured will be required to return the excess.

In *Meineke v. Twin City Fire Insurance Co.*, 892 P.2d 1365, 181 Ariz. 576 (Ariz. App.Div.1 1994), the Arizona court found, "Twin City by its conduct clearly repudiated the appraisal provision and its demand was unreasonably delayed under the circumstances. Twin City should have demanded appraisal earlier than it did. Under these circumstances, Twin City waived its right to demand an appraisal by unreasonably delaying the demand and forcing the Meinekes to file suit at the last possible moment to preserve their claim." The basis for the waiver conclusion was the delay of the insurer (who attempted to negotiate a settlement up to a year after the loss).

In Illinois, the Court of Appeal in *Hobbs v. State Farm Mutual Automobile Insurance Company*, 335 Ill.App.3d 1219, 836 N.E. 948, 297 Ill Dec 217, No. 5-01-0427 (2002), recognized that waiver of an arbitration clause is disfavored. It said that even though the insurer waited 16 months after litigation to demand appraisal, its right to appraisal should be enforced. Waiver is disfavored because of the public policy preference for conserving judicial resources through arbitration or appraisal. In concluding that Farmers Group, Inc. waived its right to invoke the appraisal clause, the court concluded that its participation in the litigation was not merely responsive.

In Florida, the Court of Appeal in *Opar v. Allstate Insurance Co.*, 751 So.2d 758 (Fla. App. Dist.1 2000), found no facts supporting a waiver and compelled the appraisal to go forward.

Appraisals are a valuable tool used by insurers and policyholders to address claim situations. Some may contend that allowing an insurer to request an appraisal at a later stage of the claims process hinders an insured's ability to reach a timely resolution of its claim. Others would contend that the insurer's right to request an appraisal reduces costs associated with potentially unnecessary litigation and reduces the incidence of fraud.

Insurers, in a dispute with the insured about the quantum of the claim always have the opportunity to resolve the issue by appraisal before litigation. As the Supreme Court of Texas noted, by so doing, the insurer may deprive the insured of any claim of bad faith if the appraisal award is less than that offered since such would be *prima facie* evidence of good faith.

Under Wisconsin law, if an agreement to arbitrate is silent on the issue of partisanship, even party-appointed arbitrators are presumed to be neutral and independent. Arguing that under the Federal Arbitration Act, party-appointed arbitrators are held to a lower standard of impartiality than umpires/neutrals. The court avoided the issue by finding that the challenged appraiser was neutral and the evidence showing partiality was not sufficient to be considered.

Appraisers must determine many matters other than the mere value of specific property produced before them for examination and appraisal. They must determine the quantity of property covered by the policy and on hand at the time of the fire, the quantity destroyed, the quantity damaged, whether the damage resulted from causes covered by the policy or from other causes not covered thereby, and various other questions, both of law and fact, upon which the parties may differ. [*Continental Ins. Co. of New York v. Titcomb*, USCA, Eighth Circuit, 7 F.2d 833 (1925)]

The appraisers have no power to determine the cause of the damage. Their power is limited to the function of determining the money value of the property which may be damaged by the storm. [*Munn v. National Fire Ins. Co of Hartford*, Supreme Court of Mississippi, 237 Miss. 641, 115 So.2d 54 (1959)]

In *Lambert v. Carneghi,* 158 Cal.App.4th 1120, 70 Cal.Rptr.3d 626, 08 Cal. Daily Op. Serv. 430, 2008 Daily Journal D.A.R. 489 (Cal. App. Dist.1 01/11/2008), the California Court of Appeal found that since an appraisal is an arbitration under California law, the appraiser is immune from suit for actions in the appraisal. "It long has been recognized that, in private arbitration proceedings, an arbitrator enjoys the benefit of an arbitral privilege because the role that he or she exercises is analogous to that of a judge. ... This rule-immunizing arbitrators in private contractual arbitration proceedings from tort liability-is well established in California. [Citation.]" There is no reason why an appraiser who is required by statute to be "disinterested" should be subject to tort liability in connection with his role as an appraiser, given this state's preference to provide immunity to those who perform the function of resolving disputes between parties.

The remedy for arbitrator misconduct lies in a court order vacating the award just as the remedy for a trial judge's misconduct is reversal of the judgment on appeal.

## Ethics for Independent Insurance Adjusters

Independent insurance adjusters serve insurance companies who do not have sufficient claims staff to handle insurance claims on behalf of various insurers.

The professional insurance adjuster recognizes that the work of adjusting insurance claims is a profession of public trust. Independent insurance adjusters should maintain a standard of integrity that will promote the goal of building public confidence and trust in the insurance industry.

Independent insurance adjusters, and company employed insurance adjusters, should follow the following rules and standards of conduct:

- Adjusters should discharge claims responsibilities for which they possess sufficient technical competence or can acquire adequate training.

- Adjusters should seek only information they believe to be relevant, timely and accurate.

- Adjusters should use only legal and ethical means of obtaining information.

- Adjusters should handle claims with no intent to mislead or misinform.

- Adjusters should be sensitive to rights of individuals to privacy.

- Respecting the right of privacy, the adjuster will take reasonable measures to protect sensitive information from illegal or unauthorized examination.

- Adjusters should avoid illegal discrimination.

- Adjusters should strive to keep personal feelings and prejudices from influencing their judgment.

- Adjusters should maintain a courteous and sensitive attitude in their interactions with insureds and claimants, seeking to understand their concerns during times of distress.

- Adjusters should assist insureds in presenting and documenting their losses, and will not place the interests of the insurer above those of the insured.

- Adjusters should maintain their business relationships with others in a manner that will promote the goal of bringing credit and honor to the profession.

- Adjusters should have no undisclosed financial interest in any direct or indirect aspect of an adjusting transaction.

- Adjusters should obey the laws and regulations related to handling claims.

- Adjusters should resist fraudulent, unmeritorious or exaggerated claims, and support public and industry organizations involved in the detection and prevention of insurance fraud.

- Adjusters should seek out all available alternatives to litigation to resolve issues in an expeditious and conciliatory manner.

- Adjusters should approach investigations and adjustments with an unprejudiced and open mind and a determination to be fair with insured and insurer.

- Adjusters should make truthful and unbiased reports of facts as discovered.

- Adjusters should assume an unvarying attitude of fairness and by competence, integrity and respect for the person with whom they deal, to promote goodwill toward the business of insurance.

- Adjusters should resist influence tending to promote improper and extravagant settlements.

- Adjusters should avoid improper alliances.

- Adjusters should refrain from improper solicitation of business.

- Adjusters should be alert to changes in policy forms and methods in order to render the highest quality of service.

- Adjusters should work for economy of expense and equitable bills for service.

- Adjusters should serve the business of insurance with loyalty and cooperate with insurers and their designated representatives in the proper handling of claims and losses.

- Adjusters should work in harmony with one another and their clients so as to foster cordial relationships among themselves and with the insurance fraternity.[1]

The professional insurance adjuster follows standards like those stated above to maintain the quality of the profession and to deal with insurance claims ethically and in good faith. Often the insurer's adjuster is asked to deal with a Public Insurance Adjuster who acts as the adjuster for the insured as the independent adjuster or company adjuster acts for the insurer.

[1] Adapted from the code of ethics of the Association of Registered Professional Adjusters [http://www.rpa-adjuster.com/ethics.html] and the California Association of Independent Insurance Adjusters [http://caiia.com/index.php?about.html]

The contact between the two should be professional and ethical. Rarely the contact between the professional adjuster and the public insurance adjuster is adversarial. Both should be working toward the same goal, the payment of proper and complete indemnity to the insured.

In Oklahoma, it was found that a disbarred or suspended lawyer needed to be prohibited from negotiating insurance claim settlements, including but not limited to, as a private insurance adjuster.[2] The court concluded that the disbarment took the lawyer out of the ability to treat an insured with the utmost good faith and refused to issue a license as a public insurance adjuster.

In Florida, unprofessional conduct of attorney occurring during his employment as an insurance adjuster and not as a practicing attorney nevertheless warranted his disbarment.[3]

The bar should conduct its own investigations, and the energy at the disposal of the Association of Casualty and Surety Companies might better be utilized in perfecting a code of ethics for insurance adjusters and in enforcing it, in as much as it is a matter of common knowledge, that activities of certain adjusters tend to breed the sort of unprofessional conduct alleged in the complaint filed in *Schoolfield v. Bean*, 26 Tenn.App. 30, 167 S.W.2d 359 and *State ex rel. Turner v. Denman*, 36 Tenn.App. 613, 259 S.W.2d 891.

## Public Adjusters Ethics

Public Adjusters are claims professionals who are employed exclusively by a policyholder who has sustained an insured first party property loss. The public

---

[2]  *In re Reinstatement of Blake,* 371 P.3d 465, 2016 OK 33 (2016)

[3]  *State ex rel Florida Bar v. Clements,* 131 So.2d 198 (1961)

adjuster handles every detail of the claim, working closely with the insured to provide the most equitable and prompt settlement possible.

The conduct of the public adjuster is governed, in most states, by statute. For example, the state of California uses the following statutes to regulate the business of a public insurance adjuster starting at §§ 15000 et seq of the Insurance Code and presented in full in Appendix 1. As a licensing statute, it attempts to require a public insurance adjuster to act ethically and in good faith on behalf of his or her client.

To perform the duties imposed upon a public adjuster to properly represent an insured should inspect the loss site immediately, analyzes the damages, assemble claim support data, review the insured's coverage, determine current replacement costs and exclusively serves the client, not the insurance company while working ethically with the insurer's adjuster.

The National Association of Public Insurance Adjusters (NAPIA) publishes a code of conduct which sets forth the ethical standards that all public insurance adjusters should follow. It provides:

The following Rules of Professional Conduct and Ethics are applicable to all members of the NAPIA:

1. The members shall conduct themselves in a spirit of fairness and justice to their clients, the Insurance Companies, and the public.

2. Members shall refrain from improper solicitation.

3. No misrepresentation of any kind shall be made to an assured or to the Insurance Companies.

4. Commission rates shall be fair and equitable, and strictly in accordance with the prevailing custom

in the locality, and must, where laws or regulations of insurance departments exist, comply fully with such laws or regulations.

5. Members shall conduct themselves so as to command respect and confidence. They shall work in harmony with one another, with their clients, and the Insurance Companies' representatives, so as to foster a cordial and harmonious relationship with all branches of the insurance business, and with the general public.

6. Members must be fitted, by knowledge and experience, for the work they undertake. They must not endanger the interests of the public adjusting profession, or risk injustice to assureds or to the Insurance Companies, by attempting to handle losses or claims for which they are not qualified, and for which they cannot find competent technical assistance.

7. Members shall not engage in the unauthorized practice of law.

8. Members shall not acquire any interest in salvaged property or participate in any way, directly or indirectly, in the reconstruction, repair or restoration of damaged property, except with the knowledge, consent and permission of the assured.

9. Members shall be cooperative and assist one another in every possible way.

10. Members shall not disseminate or use any form of agreement, advertising, or any printed matter that is harmful to the profession of public adjusting, or which does not comply with the rules and regulations of the Insurance Department of the state in which such member is professionally

engaged, or which might subject public adjusting and public adjusters to criticism or disrespect.[4]

In Texas, Insurance code §19.713 states that the requirements for public insurance adjusters include: conducting their business "fairly and in good faith without detriment to the public," refraining from improper solicitation, refraining from using misrepresentations in the conduct of their business. Texas prohibits a public adjuster charging inappropriate fees and commissions, not completing continuing education, and requiring that the public adjuster possesses adequate knowledge and experience to handle their work appropriately.

The public adjuster should not engage in the unauthorized practice of law, not engage in activities that may be construed as presenting a conflict of interest or obtaining a financial interest in salvaged property that is the subject of a claim, nor should the public adjuster use advertisements that violate the Insurance Code. The public adjuster must use contract forms that are approved by the commissioner.

An example of less than appropriate action by a public insurance adjuster and the lawyer who represented the same client, involved a claim for the 1994 Northridge earthquake that resulted in claims of multiple wrongful claims handling. The 1994 Northridge, California earthquake caused billions of dollars in damages across Southern California.

Hundreds of millions of dollars of time barred insurance claims that were reinstated by a state statute, drew lawyers and public adjusters seeking large contingent fees. Some public adjusters charging larger contingent fees than lawyers thereby making it impossible for the

4   http://www.napia.com/learn/code-conduct.asp, in addition, Florida Public Adjusters post a code of ethics at http://www.fapia.net/bylaws.html.

insured to effectuate repairs after paying the contingent fee.

Investigation was limited and because of the catastrophe many unnecessary and spurious suits were filed. Insurance fraud was rampant and insurers paid rather than fight. In addition, insurers denied claims they should not have denied because of their staff being unable to deal with the high volume of claims without making an error and the need to return special storm adjusters back to their homes.

Their errors caused the state of California after it passed a law allowing insureds to sue their insurers as late as 2002, four years after expiration of the statute and eight years after expiration of the private limitations of action provision of most policies. This change in the limitation period brought about many proper suits and some spurious actions.

In an unpublished opinion, the California Court of Appeal dealt a serious blow to an attorney who filed an apparently malicious and unfounded lawsuit against Scottsdale Insurance Company (Scottsdale). The Court of Appeal decided that an attorney must stand trial on an action from an insurer for malicious prosecution because it was highly probable that the suit would be successful.[5]

In bringing the action Scottsdale took an important step that will protect insurers against lawyers and public adjusters who use the courts as a bludgeon and act unethically. No party nor their lawyer or public adjuster should ever force insurers to litigate a claim for the sole purpose of forcing the insurer to pay to avoid the costs of litigation. If they take the case to trial and prove the malice a punitive damages award against the lawyer and the public adjuster will go far to chill the proclivity of

---

[5]  *Scottsdale Insurance Co. v. Zelig*, 2008 WL 962921, No. B181761, 2006.CA.0003625 (Cal.App. Dist.2 05/02/2006)

some lawyers to file suit without sufficient facts on the assumption that everything an insurer does is wrong and in bad faith.

Unfortunately, California law only allows bad faith damages against an insurer and refuses to allow an insurer to collect damages for the tortious bad faith conduct of an insured. However, if an insured acts fraudulently or maliciously the insured can be sued for fraud or malicious prosecution.

The action against Scottsdale Insurance Company began in 1994 after the Northridge earthquake when Regency Royale Homeowners Association (Regency) claimed it sustained damage. Five months later, Regency submitted an application to Scottsdale for earthquake insurance and represented that it was insured through Homestead Insurance Company and had sustained no losses during the previous five years. Scottsdale relied on those representations in issuing a policy to Regency providing coverage from July 1, 1994 to July 1, 1995.

On December 26, 2001, Regency's public insurance adjuster, Kapilow & Son (Kapilow), requested that Scottsdale assign an adjuster to investigate Regency's claim of earthquake damage under the policy even though it was not in effect at the time of the earthquake. On December 31, 2001, Zelig filed suit in Los Angeles Superior Court against Scottsdale on behalf of Regency, entitled *Waldman et al. v. Golden Bear et al.*, case No. BC265308 (Waldman) claiming that Scottsdale insured Regency at the time of the earthquake and owed Regency indemnity.

The complaint was filed under a statute that revived time-barred Northridge earthquake insurance claims provided the insured had contacted his insurer prior to January 1, 2000. The lawsuit was filed prior to January 1, 2002. Zelig was provided the Regency file from Kapilow with what he claimed were insufficient time prior to the filing deadline under the revival statute to undertake an independent investigation of whether Scottsdale was the proper insurer.

Zelig claimed he relied on Kapilow's representation that Scottsdale insured Regency for the earthquake risk in filing the complaint. Kapilow likewise had not independently investigated whether Scottsdale was the proper insurer. In January 2002, Scottsdale informed Kapilow that Regency's policy did not provide coverage until six months after the Northridge earthquake and that Homestead Insurance was likely the proper insurer.

Scottsdale also advised Zelig and Kapilow that Regency had not initiated a claim prior to January 1, 2000 as required under the revival statute. Regardless, Zelig served the complaint on Scottsdale on July 8, 2002. In October 2002 Scottsdale responded to Regency's request for documents in part by producing the declarations page of the insurance policy it had issued to Regency for inception six months after the earthquake.

In November 2002, Kapilow informed Zelig's office that Farmers and State Farm carried coverage on the Regency property at the time of the earthquake. Scottsdale had additional communications with Zelig in April and July asserting it had not insured the risk of the earthquake since its policy was issued after the earthquake.

After Scottsdale filed its motion for summary judgment, new counsel, associated in on behalf of Regency, acknowledged that Scottsdale was not the proper insurer. That counsel dismissed Scottsdale without prejudice before the summary judgment hearing. Scottsdale incurred in excess of $30,000 in attorney fees in the evaluation and defense of the Waldman action. The trial court held that the voluntary dismissal without prejudice in the prior action was a favorable termination sufficient to support a suit by Scottsdale against Zelig, Kapilow and Regency for the tort of malicious prosecution.

The court concluded that evidence that reflects "the opinion of the prosecuting party that, if pursued, the action would result in a decision in favor of the defendant is evidence of a favorable termination. [*Minasian v. Sapse* (1978) 80 Cal.App.3d 823, 827] By demonstrating that during the pendency of Scottsdale's motion for summary judgment new counsel for Regency dismissed the complaint. Coupled with the evidence tending to show that Scottsdale was not the proper insurer, this dismissal reflected on the merits of the case.

The court found such information damning and was satisfied that a "favorable termination" was demonstrated by Scottsdale. The court found that Zelig waived his argument about no probable cause or malice by providing no facts or law to back his contentions on appeal. The essence of allegations of Scottsdale's suit was malicious prosecution.

The suit also claimed that Zelig and Kapilow conspired to commit a malicious prosecution that resulted in damage to Scottsdale. These allegations are sufficient to state a cause of action against Zelig.

The trial went forward and made clear. Zelig, Kapilow and their client were looking at a probable judgment for $30,000 in attorneys' fees and as much as nine times that amount in punitive damages. Scottsdale properly took an aggressive stand against a lawyer and public adjuster who they believe so blatantly abused the process of the court and maliciously forced Scottsdale to defend a lawsuit that could not possibly succeed.

Scottsdale gave Zelig and Kapilow the opportunity to avoid the suit by informing them of the true nature of the policy, the Scottsdale policy's effective dates and that it would be impossible for it to respond with indemnity to a claim for damages occurring before the policy came into effect, was kind. Kindness was returned with aggression. Scottsdale's reasonable conduct and attempt to resolve the situation in a non-confrontational, ethical manner was rewarded by abuse, unethical behavior and a refusal by Zelig to be confused with facts.

The Court of Appeal was neither confused nor cowed. The results of the trial would have been interesting but the defendants settled and it did not go to trial. Another appeal resulted when the settlement amount was not paid.

Insurers victimized by similar spurious lawsuits should consider seeking a return of their costs against those who brought the suit as did Scottsdale insurance. The full text of the case, and parts of the subsequent appeal, are in the Appendix 1.

About a year later the same Court of Appeal, clearly upset with the parties, held in *Scottsdale Insurance Co. v. Zelig*, No. B199812 (Cal.App. Dist.2 04/10/2008) that in the third appeal filed by appellant Steven L. Zelig (Zelig) in the malicious prosecution case against his sole proprietorship, The Law Offices of Steven L. Zelig (Law Offices) was contumacious.

Without citing any authority, Zelig asserted that he cannot be added to the judgment because he was released by the settlement agreement. Zelig ignored the evidence favorable to the trial court's ruling. The parties' settlement agreement, as reflected on the record, specifically provided that the release of liability was conditioned on the payment of $45,000 by Law Offices of Steven L. Zelig, Zelig's sole proprietorship. Since the payment condition was never satisfied, Zelig cannot claim to have been released. To countenance Zelig's argument-that a settlement releases a party even though the monetary consideration was never paid – would render settlement agreements meaningless.

Scottsdale filed a motion for sanctions against Zelig for the filing of a frivolous appeal. The court conclude that the appeal was filed for the improper purpose of delaying the effect of the judgment adverse to Zelig and of avoiding and delaying payment of a settlement obligation agreed to by Zelig in a judicially supervised settlement. The court also concluded that it further appeared to be part of a continuing pattern of conduct throughout this case in which Zelig has abused the legal system through delay and obstruction.

The court concluded that the appeal also indisputably had no merit and added a sanction of $8,250 against Zelig and in favor of Scottsdale.

A lawyer and the client that maliciously prosecute a spurious lawsuit should pay damages to those they harm. Bringing a suit against an insurer whose policy was not in effect at the time of the loss is evidence conduct that the ethical public adjuster and ethical lawyer would want to avoid.

It appears clear, therefore, that all people involved in the business of insurance claims handling express the highest ethical standards in providing a service to an insured person who incurs an insured loss.

The conduct of Zelig and Kapilow were, as the court found, unethical. As a result of their unethical conduct the case against Scottsdale was dismissed and both were sanctioned by the court and required to pay the attorneys fees incurred by Scottsdale. When an attorney or a public insurance adjuster acts unethically every insurer involved should do everything possible to punish their actions as Scottsdale did to Kapilow and Zelig.

Cases like the *Scottsdale* case and its progeny have given a bad name to the public insurance adjusting industry and the practice of law.

Most public adjusters are professional insurance adjusters who work in accordance with the ethical requirements of the National Association of Public Insurance Adjusters. Some, like Mr. Kapilow did with regard to the Regency case, do not. The ethical insurance professional acting for an insurer with a public adjuster should deal with the public adjuster professionally and ethically. If the public adjuster does not do the same it might be useful to retain counsel to protect the insurer.

Most lawyers act in accordance with the ethical requirements of the bar. Filing suit against a party the lawyer knows, or should know, had no obligation to the plaintiff is a clear breach of those ethical standards as the trial and appellate courts found Zelig breached with regard to the Regency or Waldman action against Scottsdale.

## A Reason to Do Away with the Tort of Bad Faith

Catastrophes, like hurricanes, bring out the best and worst of the U.S. public. The Cajun Navy coming to the rescue of flood victims without a need for remuneration and seeking nothing more than thanks shows the best of the U.S. public. Those who attempt to profit from a catastrophe and steal from an insurer and seeking bad faith tort damages in addition to actual losses should be condemned and shunned.

In *Ammar Investments, LLC d/b/a Zegar, Inc. and d/b/a Fouad & Faris, Inc. v. Certain Underwriters Of Lloyd's, London*, No. 18-ca-347, Fifth Circuit Court of Appeal State of Louisiana (December 12, 2018) the Louisiana Court of Appeal not only refused to allow the attempt to profit from a hurricane but chided those attempting to profit from the storm. The only thing the appellate court failed to do was to report the plaintiff to a prosecutor for prosecution for attempted insurance fraud.

FACTS

Ammar Investments, LLC d/b/a Zegar, Inc. and d/b/a Fouad & Faris, Inc. ("AI"), appealed the trial court's judgment awarding it $26,654.10 in damages for loss of personal property as a result of Hurricane Isaac, but denying its claim for damages sustained to the roof of its building. AI also appealed the trial court's denial of its motion for new trial and/or rehearing of a prior judgment granting summary judgment in favor of defendant, Certain Underwriters of Lloyd's, London ("Underwriters"), and dismissing AI's claim for bad faith damages due to Underwriters' alleged misrepresentation of its policy provisions pertaining to the hurricane deductible.

Ammar Zughayer is the owner of AI, which owns and operates Mike's Food Mart, a convenience store and gas station located on River Road East in Garyville, Louisiana. Mike's Food Mart was insured against building and personal property (inventory) loss under a policy of insurance issued to AI by Underwriters ("the Policy"). The Policy, which required a three percent (3%) wind and hail deductible, was effective from June 8, 2012 to June 8, 2013; its coverage included a $300,000.00 limit for damages occasioned to the building, and a $200,000.00 limit for loss of personal property located on the premises.

On August 28-29, 2012, Hurricane Isaac made landfall in St. John the Baptist Parish causing widespread power outages throughout the parish. Underwriters retained SyNerGy Adjusting Corporation to investigate Mr. Zughayer's claims. SyNerGy's senior claims' adjuster, Mike Dossett, inspected the property and assessed the damages. He discovered only minimal damage to the metal fascia of the canopy situated over the diesel pumps. Mr. Dossett then inspected the inside of the building, which he found to be in good condition and well-stocked. Mr. Zughayer identified for him two areas of the store where he claimed water was leaking through the roof: (1) in between a walk-in cooler and a back wall, and (2) around a hood vent positioned over cooking equipment in the kitchen. Mr. Zughayer then showed Mr. Dossett the store's inventory that was damaged, which included food and drinks that were spoiled as a result of the power outage.

Mr. Dossett found the building to be in "excellent condition" and determined that the covered damages to the premises were minor. No estimates for building damages, nor a completed itemized list of damaged contents, were ever provided by Mr. Zughayer to Mr. Dossett during the adjustment period.

Although it did not send new or detailed information required AI filed suit against Underwriters seeking recovery for damages to the building and personal property (i.e., business inventory) caused by Hurricane Isaac. AI sought additional damages claiming that Underwriters acted in bad faith and was "arbitrary and capricious" in adjusting its claim and refusing to pay for its property damage. The matter proceeded to a two-day trial after which the trial court took the matter under advisement and later issued judgment with written reasons. The trial court denied AI's claim for damages to the building on the basis that AI failed to adduce sufficient evidence to satisfy its burden of proving that damages were sustained to the building's roof, canopies or signs.

Despite its rejection of AI's claim for damages to the building's roof caused by the hurricane, the trial court awarded $26,654.10 to AI for the cost of replacing its water-damaged tobacco inventory (less the 3% hurricane deductible), which was stored in the attic directly underneath the roof.

## LAW AND DISCUSSION

To prevail on a claim for bad faith claims adjusting a plaintiff bears the burden of proving:

1. the insured provided a proof of loss;

2. the proof of loss was satisfactory; that is, sufficient information to allow the adjuster to pay the undisputed amount within 30 days; and

3. the insurer's failure to timely make payment of the undisputed amount was the result of conduct that was arbitrary, capricious and/or without probable cause.

An insurer's actions are "arbitrary and capricious" when its willful refusal of a claim is not based on a good faith defense, or is unreasonable or without probable cause.

AI argues that the uncontroverted testimony at trial established that at the time of Hurricane Isaac, the building and its roof were just over a year old and that there had been no prior issues with leaks. AI introduced numerous photographs into evidence at trial that were taken of the inside of the convenience store by Mr. Zughayer depicting what he alleged to be water damage caused by the leaking roof. Notably, of the 82 photographs offered into evidence, not one photograph was taken of the purported damage to the roof.

Although A-1's estimate was submitted to Mr. Zughayer on September 28, 2012—only twenty days after Mr. Dossett had inspected the building on behalf of Underwriters—this estimate was never provided to Underwriters (nor was any other estimate of purported damage to the building or its contents).

In Louisiana, a plaintiff bears the burden of proving with legal certainty every item of damages, and the plaintiff's own uncorroborated testimony is insufficient to satisfy that burden. If the damaged property has been restored to its former condition by repair, the proper basis for assessing damages is the repair bill itself.

The trial judge determined AI failed to produce a single receipt for the repairs to the roof. Further, the check Mr. Zughayer claims to have given to Mr. Burr as evidence that roof repairs were made — which check Mr. Burr denied ever having even seen it — was made payable to someone other than Mr. Burr and was made out for $28,200.00, not the estimated $27,000.00. The only consistency in the testimony of Mr. Zughayer and Mr. Burr was that Mr. Burr was paid $22,000.00 in cash for the job, yet neither could produce a single receipt, bank statement or deposit slip as proof that the cash payment was either made or received.

When Underwriters subsequently sought to subpoena AI's (or Mr. Zughayer's) bank records, those checks that AI claimed to have been paid did not appear. Nor did the bank's records reveal cash withdrawals matching the amounts indicated on the checks.

Given AI's presentation of its case in the trial court — which the lower court found to be "contradictory [and] inconsistent" — coupled with the total absence of documentary evidence to substantiate the damages AI alleged were sustained to the building's canopies, gas pumps, and air conditioning units, it is understandable why the trial court rejected all of AI's claims to the building (including the roof).

Underwriters filed a cross appeal in this matter averring the trial court manifestly erred in awarding $26,654.10 in damages to AI for the loss of its tobacco inventory. Because AI's evidence regarding its tobacco inventory loss was riddled with conflicting, inconsistent and unsupported evidence that was insufficient to prove that the alleged damage was in any way related to Hurricane Isaac, the appellate court resolved the inconsistency in favor of Underwriters. Consequently, it reversed that portion of the trial court's judgment awarding $26,654.10 to AI for loss of its tobacco inventory.

Not only did Mr. Zughayer fail to show Mr. Dossett damaged tobacco that day, Mr. Zughayer failed to even mention water damage to his tobacco inventory. The appellate court found it incredible that having placed a substantial order that same day to replace inventory he was claiming to be damaged, and at a significant cost for which he was requesting repayment, that when asked to specify the damaged items, he would fail to even mention the loss of that expensive item.

AI's burden to show a preponderance of the evidence of a loss to tobacco products was manifestly erroneous and clearly wrong requires reversal of the $26,654.10 in damages awarded to AI for its loss of inventory claim.

## ZALMA OPINION

The lawsuit filed by AI and Zughayer was more than inadequate it was clearly fraudulent and supported by false documents. Insurance fraud is a felony in Louisiana and La.R.S. 22:1243 makes it a crime to present or cause to be presented any written or oral statement as part of or in support of a claim for payment or other benefit pursuant to an insurance policy, knowing that such statement contains any false, incomplete, or fraudulent information concerning any fact or thing material to such claim. As a result the insurer is obligated to report AI and Zughayer to the state's insurance fraud investigators and the trial judge and court of appeal should have recommended prosecution.

## Duty to Defend Only Applies to Person Sued

### No Right to Rescind a Contract that Does Not Exist

Liability insurance is designed to provide defense and indemnity to persons insured who are sued as a result of events covered by the insurance policy. It does not, nor can it, provide defense to a person not insured. Further, a liability policy will not defend if a clear and unambiguous exclusion applies.

In *Robert Mau; Eagle Well Services, Inc. v. Twin City Fire Insurance Co.*, No. 17-3392, United States Court of Appeals For the Eighth Circuit (December 6, 2018) Robert Mau and Eagle Well Services, Inc. ("EWS") failed in its efforts to get defense and indemnity from Twin City. They then appealed the district court's grant of Twin City Fire Insurance Company's ("Twin City") cross-motion for summary judgment.

### THE AVAILABLE COVERAGE

Twin City insured Eagle Operating, Inc. and its subsidiaries. Endorsement No. 2 of the policy defined Eagle Operating's subsidiaries to include EWS and MW Industries, Inc. During the relevant period, Mau was president of Eagle Operating, shareholder and president of EWS, director and president of MW, and an owner of American Well Services ("AWS").

In February 2012, EWS sold its assets to a predecessor of Sun Well Services ("Sun Well") through an Asset Purchase Agreement ("Agreement"). EWS and Mau were parties to the Agreement, which included a noncompetition covenant.

### BREACH OF A NONCOMPETITION CONTRACT

After the Agreement was signed, MW sold equipment to AWS. Claiming that the sale violated the noncompetition covenant, Sun Well sued Mau for breach of contract, fraud, and civil conspiracy, and it sued EWS for breach of contract and fraud. Twin City refused to defend the suit.

## THE DECLARATORY RELIEF ACTION

Mau and EWS sued Twin City, seeking a declaration that they were insured under the policy. They also sued Twin City for breach of contract and breach of the implied covenant of good faith and fair dealing. Mau filed a motion for partial summary judgment. Twin City filed a response in opposition and a cross-motion for summary judgment, asking the court to find that Twin City had no duty to defend Mau or EWS. The district court denied Mau's motion for partial summary judgment, and it granted Twin City's cross-motion for summary judgment.

North Dakota law applies in this case. An insurer has no duty to defend an action if there is no possibility of coverage under the policy. Any doubt about whether a duty to defend exists must be resolved in favor of the insured.

Mau argued before the district court that Twin City owed him a duty to defend because Sun Well sued him in his capacity as a director and officer of MW, an insured subsidiary of Eagle Operating. The district court rejected his argument. Sun Well's claims do not depend on any actions Mau took as president of MW. This is evidenced by the fact that Sun Well did not sue MW. While Sun Well's complaint mentions MW contextually, MW is not a party to the suit. There is no need for an insurer to defend a party who was not sued.

Instead, Sun Well's claims depend on the alleged breach of the noncompetition covenant in the Agreement between EWS and Sun Well, an agreement to which MW was not a party. Sun Well would have no claim for breach of contract, fraud, or civil conspiracy against Mau were it not for the Agreement, which he signed as president of EWS, not as a director and officer of MW. Thus, Sun Well sued Mau in his capacity as president of EWS. Because Sun Well's complaint contains no claims based on any actions Mau took as a director and officer of MW, Twin City owes him no duty to defend on that basis.

Eagle Operating's insurance policy with Twin City includes an exclusion that applies to Mau in his capacity as president of EWS. The dual service exclusion provides as follows: "The Insurer shall not pay Loss: . . . of an Insured Person based upon, arising from, or in any way related to such Insured Person's service, at any time, as a director, officer, trustee, regent, governor or equivalent executive or as an employee of any entity other than an Insured Entity even if such service is at the direction or request of such Insured Entity...."

Because the allegations of the complaint govern the duty to defend, the appellate court looks to Sun Well's complaint when applying the dual service exclusion. The complaint says that Mau "participated in the formation and subsequent operation" of AWS. And it says that AWS is an "affiliate" of Mau "as that term is defined in Section 7.13 of the [Agreement]." Any loss Mau suffers from the Sun Well litigation certainly "arises from" and is "related to" his service in one of the exclusion's stipulated roles for AWS, an uninsured entity. Thus, the dual service exclusion applies to Mau.

Because Mau was not sued in his capacity as director and officer of MW and because the dual service exclusion applies, there is no possibility of coverage for Mau under Twin City's policy.

Similarly, Twin City has no duty to defend EWS in this suit. The insurance policy includes another exclusion that reads as follows: "The Insurer shall not pay Loss under Insuring Agreement (C) in connection with any Claim based upon, arising from, or in any way related to any actual or alleged: ¶ (1) liability under any contract or agreement, provided that this exclusion shall not apply to the extent that liability would have been incurred in the absence of such contract or agreement . . . ."

In other words, the contract exclusion applies to claims arising from the insured's contracts or agreements unless liability otherwise would exist in the absence of the contract or agreement. This exclusion applies to EWS because Sun Well's claims against EWS for breach of contract and fraud are based upon, arise from, or are related to the Agreement, and liability could not have been incurred in the absence of the Agreement.

EWS does not contest that Sun Well's claims are based upon, arise from, or are related to the Agreement. EWS argues that Sun Well's fraud claim created the possibility that the Agreement would be rescinded. If the Agreement were to be rescinded, EWS claims, liability would exist in the absence of the Agreement.

In either case, even if EWS's arguments had some validity, the contract exclusion would apply to any resulting liability. Sun Well's fraud claim would not exist in the absence of the Agreement. The fraud claim alleged that Mau and EWS "concealed" material facts about their plan to breach the noncompetition covenant that they had a duty to disclose. And a contract that does not exist cannot be rescinded.

There is no possibility of coverage for EWS under Twin City's policy because the contract exclusion applies.

Applying North Dakota law, the court held that Twin City owed no duty to defend Mau in his capacity as director and officer of MW because no claims were brought against him in that capacity and, in any event, the dual service exclusion applied. The court also held that Twin City did not owe a duty to defend EWS where the claims against it for breach of contract and fraud are based upon the Asset Purchase Agreement and liability could not have been incurred in absence of the Agreement. Furthermore, even if EWS's arguments had some validity, the contract exclusion would apply to any resulting liability.

ZALMA OPINION

Liability insurance is not designed to protect against breaches of contracts which, by definition, must be neither contingent nor unknown losses and are, therefore, not insurable. Breaching a non-competition clause is, by definition, an intentional act. Since fortuity is required for coverage under a liability policy an intentional breach of contract can never be the subject of insurance. Finally, there can never be an obligation of an insurer to do the impossible – defend an insured who was not sued.

## Suit Must Allege Facts Giving Rise to a Potential for Coverage

### Facts Ultimately Proven in the Underlying Litigation Have No Bearing on an Insurer's Duty to Defend

In Maryland and many other states coverage for defense or indemnity are determined from the allegations in the suit brought against the insured for which it seeks defense and indemnity. A declaratory relief suit seeks an order from the court that the insurer owes the insured defense or defense and indemnity. The pleading of the declaratory relief suit and the underlying action control the decision.

In *Robert A. Casero, Jr.; Catherine Mary Hattenburg v. Chicago Title Insurance Company; Fidelity National Title Group, Inc.,* No. 18-1234, United States Court of Appeals for the Fourth Circuit (December 11, 2018) the Appellants, Robert A. Casero, Jr. and Catherine Mary Hattenburg, appealed the district court's orders granting the Appellees' (Chicago's and Fidelity's) motion to dismiss the declaratory relief complaint and denying reconsideration. The suit asked the court to render a declaratory judgment that the Appellees had a duty under a title insurance policy to defend and indemnify the Appellants from various claims asserted by their neighbors.

## DECISION

On review the Fourth Circuit Court of Appeals must assume all well-pled facts to be true, and draw all reasonable inferences in favor of the plaintiff. Under Maryland law, which is applicable here, in determining whether an insurer has a duty to defend, a court must determine the coverage under the terms of the policy and determine whether the allegations in the underlying complaint bring the claim within the policy's coverage.

The inquiry focuses on the language and requirements of the policy and the allegations of the underlying suit. The facts ultimately proven in the underlying litigation have no bearing on an insurer's duty to defend.

A court determines whether there is any potentiality of coverage, i.e. whether the allegations in the complaint could possibly give rise to coverage under the policy. The duty to defend is broader than the duty to indemnify and arises when allegations of a law suit demonstrate any claim potentially covered by policy. Where a potentiality of coverage is uncertain from the allegations of a complaint, any doubt must be resolved in favor of the insured.

The Fourth Circuit thoroughly reviewed the record and the relevant legal authorities and concluded that the district court did not err in concluding that, based on the allegations of the underlying complaint, there was no potentiality of coverage under the policy. Therefore, the Appellees had no duty to defend the Appellants in the underlying suit.

## ZALMA OPINION

Appellate pleadings are called "briefs" but are seldom brief. Appellate decisions often emulate the briefs filed by the lawyers by being anything but brief. The Fourth Circuit refused to follow the rule of thumb and issued a truly brief decision that found no potentiality for coverage and, therefore, no need for the insurers to defend.

## Coulda, Shoulda, Woulda – Divorce is Expensive

### Divorce Effects Cancellation of Dependent Life Insurance Coverage

Employer provided life insurance programs are controlled by the Employee Retirement Income Security Act ("ERISA") and its terms and conditions. Unlike insurance obtained directly by the insured for the benefit of a beneficiary the ERISA policy provides limited coverages for which the employee/insured has no control.

In *David Glenn Morris v. Southern Intermodal Xpress, Assurant Employee Benefits, Union Security Insurance Company*, No. 18-10785, United States Court of Appeals for the Eleventh Circuit (December 4, 2018) David Morris filed a federal civil action to recover benefits allegedly due him under a life-insurance policy governed by ERISA.

Morris sued both Southern Intermodal Xpress ("SIX"), which offered the policy to its employees, and Union Security Insurance Company ("Union"), which issued the policy and then denied Morris benefits under the trade name Assurant Employee Benefits. The district court liberally construed his complaint as bringing a claim for wrongful denial of benefits under an ERISA plan, pursuant to 29 U.S.C. § 1132(a)(1)(B); dismissed the complaint as to SIX for lack of a connection to the decision to deny benefits; and then granted summary judgment in favor of Union on the merits of Morris's claim.

### THE INSURANCE

Morris was insured under a group term-life-insurance policy offered by his employer, SIX, and issued by Union. The policy insured Morris's life and also provided dependent life-insurance benefits. Dependent insurance extended to "eligible dependents," which the policy defined as a "lawful spouse" and certain children. Dependent insurance ended if, among other things, a dependent was "no longer eligible." Morris was married at the time he became insured, but he divorced on September 24, 2015. Nearly two months later, his ex-wife died.

FACTS

After his ex-wife's death, Morris filed a claim for dependent life-insurance benefits under the policy. Union denied the claim because, in its view, dependent coverage ended as of the date of divorce. At the time of her death, according to Union, Morris's ex-wife was not his lawful spouse and so was not an eligible dependent under the policy.

Morris then sued both SIX and Union "pursuant to . . . ERISA," demanding payment of the "death beneficiary proceeds" related to his ex-wife's death. He claimed that he was entitled to benefits as the "named beneficiary." He attached to his complaint a copy of the policy and a letter from Union denying his appeal.

SIX moved to dismiss the complaint for failure to state a claim. SIX argued that it could not be held responsible for wrongful denial of benefits because, as the documents Morris submitted with his complaint demonstrated, it had no role in denying benefits. Rather, SIX asserted, Morris's claim was against Union alone. Union filed an answer and then moved for summary judgment.

Morris's complaint did not identify a specific ERISA provision as the basis for his claim. But given his allegations that he was wrongfully denied benefits under an "ERISA policy," the district court liberally construed his complaint as raising a claim under 29 U.S.C. § 1132(a)(1)(B), which authorizes an ERISA-plan "participant or beneficiary" to sue "to recover benefits due to him under the terms of his plan, to enforce his rights under the terms of the plan, or to clarify his rights to future benefits under the terms of the plan."

The district court then granted SIX's motion to dismiss. Later, the district court granted summary judgment to Union, determining that Union correctly denied the claim under the terms of the life-insurance policy. The court reasoned that dependent life-insurance coverage for Morris's ex-wife had ended before her death because she was no longer his "lawful spouse" as of the date of divorce.

## ANALYSIS

Morris argues that the district court erred in forcing him to proceed under 29 U.S.C. § 1132(a)(1)(B), that he stated a plausible claim against SIX because SIX offered the policy under which, in Morris's view, benefits were owed, and that the court erred by failing to compel SIX to pay dependent benefits following the death of his ex-wife.

First, the district court did not err by liberally construing Morris's complaint to raise a claim under 29 U.S.C. § 1132(a)(1)(B). That provision of ERISA authorizes a participant in or beneficiary of an ERISA plan to bring a civil action "to recover benefits due to him under the terms of his plan." 29 U.S.C. § 1132(a)(1)(B). Because Morris filed suit "pursuant to . . . ERISA" to recover "death beneficiary proceeds" he claimed were owed under an "ERISA policy," the district court properly construed his claim as one "to recover benefits due to him under the terms of his plan" under § 1132(a)(1)(B). Furthermore, any state-law claim that Morris's complaint may have raised was preempted by ERISA. That provision converts state-law claims into federal ERISA claims.

Second, the district court did not err by dismissing the complaint for failure to state a claim against SIX, Morris's employer. The court concluded that SIX was not liable because nothing in the complaint indicated that the denial of benefits was caused by any impropriety on SIX's part. The court noted that the policy itself gave Union "sole discretionary authority" over the benefits decision, that Union alone issued the decision denying Morris's claim for benefits and his appeal based on its interpretation of the policy, and that Morris had not alleged any impropriety in SIX's handling of the claim paperwork before Union made its decision. The court concluded that any improper denial of benefits was attributable to Union, not to SIX.

By granting summary judgment to Union on the merits of Morris's claim for unpaid benefits, the district court determined that Union correctly denied benefits under the terms of the life insurance policy.

The Eleventh Circuit agreed with the district court that Union's decision to deny benefits was the correct one under the terms of Morris's life-insurance policy. Morris's policy provided coverage to "eligible dependent[s]," which included a "lawful spouse." Coverage ended if a dependent was no longer "eligible."

Because Morris's ex-wife was not his "lawful spouse" as of the date of their divorce, she ceased to be an "eligible" dependent as of that same date. By the time of Morris's ex-wife's death nearly two months later, any dependent coverage had ended.

Morris's assertion that he is a "named beneficiary"— in the sense that he may have been entitled to benefits notwithstanding the divorce — finds no support in the language of the policy because the ex-wife was no longer an insured or eligible for the dependent coverage.

## ZALMA OPINION

It is essential to the interpretation of an insurance policy that the court asked to interpret it read the words of the policy. In this case the clear and unambiguous language of the policy only allowed coverage for a dependent lawful spouse. Since the divorce was final she was no longer a dependent nor was she a lawful spouse. Clear language of a policy must be enforced where there is no ambiguity and in this case it was.

## Proof of Materiality of a Representation

Every rescission requires proof that the facts misrepresented or concealed was material.

Different courts have characterized the element of materiality differently. For example, in Connecticut:

> A fact is material . . . when . . . it would so increase the degree or character of the risk of the insurance so as to substantially influence its issuance, or substantially affect the rate of premium. *Davis-Scofield v. Agricultural Insurance Co.*, 109 Conn. 673 at p. 678, 145 A. 38 at p. 40 (1920).

In Indiana:

> The representations of the insured are material to the risk if a truthful answer would lead the insurer to decline issuing insurance or charge a higher premium. *Holtzclaw v. Bankers Mutual Insurance Co.*, 448 N.E. 2d 55 at p. 58 (Ind. App. 3d Dist., 1983).

In Michigan:

> As a test for determining whether a misstatement in an insurance application is material . . . a misrepresentation is material if it is such that the insurer would not have entered into the contract had it known the true facts. *Wiedmayer v. Midland Mutual Life Insurance Company*, 108 Mich. App.96 at p. 100, 310 N.W. 2d 285 at p. 286 (1981).

A key decision on what is necessary to prove that rescission was proper follows in full. It is a primer on the availability of rescission of an insurance policy and how to prove materiality is *Imperial Casualty and Indemnity Co. v. Sogomonian*, 198 Cal. App. 3d 169, 243 Cal. Rptr. 639 (Cal.App.Dist.2 02/04/1988).[6]

Mr. Sogomonian was not a nice man. He became, among others, the subject of hearings before the Congress of the United States, in S. Hrg. 104-604, May 15, 1996, *Russian Organized Crime in the United States*,[7] where some of the testimony provided included that from U.S. Customs. Had the insurers known about the information reported to the U.S. Senate they would have been more careful in their dealings with Mr. Sogomonian. The fact that the suit was resolved by proof of rescission eliminated the need for evidence of criminal activity and arson.

The author testified in the trial which, in 40 years as a litigator and expert witness, is the first and only time he observed three armed bailiffs in the courtroom who never took their hands off their weapons. In addition, after testimony was completed, the bailiff offered to escort the author safely to the elevator.

In *The Suit Gallery Five Star Men's Wear, Inc v. Granite State Insurance Company, Inc*, No. G042622 (Cal.App. Dist.4 03/09/2011) the California Court of Appeal affirmed the rescission of an insurance policy as a matter of law because of material misrepresentation of fact.

---

[6] . Although my name does not appear in the decision it consumed 15 years of the author's life with multiple lawsuits including one seeking return of the debris from the fire. Mr. Sogomonian was unsuccessful in each of his efforts.

[7] . http://www.archive.org/stream/russianorganized00unit/russianorganized00unit_djvu.txt.

In *Suit Gallery Five Star Men's Wear, Inc v. Granite State Insurance Company, Inc,* Not Reported in Cal.Rptr.3d, 2011 WL 810244, Nonpublished/Noncitable (Cal. Rules of Court, Rules 8.1105 and 8.1110, 8.1115), Cal.App. 4 Dist., March 09, 2011 (NO. G042622) Granite State Insurance Company (Granite State) insured Sam's Suit Gallery, Inc. (Sam's), a men's wear store. Following a burglary at the store, The Suit Gallery Five Star Men's Wear, Inc. (Five Star) made a $327,432.31 claim against the policy. Granite State rescinded the policy due to the insured's failure to disclose, in its insurance application, two prior burglaries at the store. His men's wear store in Placentia was burglarized in January 2002 and again in February 2002. His insurer at the time, Zurich, cancelled the insurance policy for the business. Abujoudeh then began shopping for new insurance. He disclosed the prior burglaries to State Farm, because the State Farm agent asked about prior losses. Having learned about the loss history, State Farm was unwilling to issue insurance for the Placentia men's wear store without the payment of a top dollar premium. So, Abujoudeh met with Jay Lee of EG Insurance Agency about obtaining insurance. According to Abujoudeh, Lee did not ask him for much information or enquire about prior losses. Abujoudeh decided to go with Lee's suggested insurer, AIG, purportedly the parent company of Granite State. However, at the time the policy was applied for and issued, Sam's was not actually registered either as a corporation or as a fictitious business name for Five Star.

On October 31, 2002, the men's wear store was burglarized again.

In its minute order, the court explained: "Granite State rescinded the policy because the insured company had a previous loss that Plaintiff did not disclose on the application. The Suit Gallery Five Star Men's Wear, Inc., operated a store in Placentia in 2002, and suffered two burglar[y] losses before the present one. The Application of Insurance specifically asks for any losses at the Placentia location, and the Plaintiff answered 'no.' That sort of representation is material and Defendant has shown that it was a misrepresentation. Therefore, Defendant has met its burden of showing that it properly rescinded the policy." The burden then shifts to the Plaintiff to show a triable issue of fact. Plaintiff has raised several issues as issues to be tried."

All the admissible evidence showed that Lee and EG Insurance Agency were brokers, not the agents of Granite State. If an insurance application was prepared by an insurance broker (the agent of the insured), the application's contents are the insured's responsibility.[8]

When a policyholder conceals or misrepresents a material fact on an insurance application, the insurer is entitled to rescind the policy. Each party to a contract of insurance shall communicate to the other, in good faith, all facts within his knowledge which are or which he believes to be material to the contract. Concealment, which is the neglect to communicate that which a party knows, and ought to communicate, entitles the injured party to rescind insurance. Similarly, if a representation is false in a material point the injured party is entitled to rescind the contract from the time the representation becomes false.

Five Star does not dispute that the insurance application submitted to Granite State did not disclose the prior burglaries on the property. It simply seeks to lay the blame for the nondisclosure on Lee and EG Insurance Agency, and then say that Granite State is stuck with it.

---

[8] . *LA Sound USA, Inc. v. St. Paul Fire & Marine Ins. Co.* (2007) 156 Cal.App.4th 1259, 1268.)

In New Jersey, an insurance agent's submission of documents materially misrepresenting insurance applicants' loss history in application for property insurance was binding on applicants, such that applicants remained liable for agent's material misrepresentation, regardless of whether that misrepresentation was intentional or innocent; signature line of application signed by applicants warned against fraudulent insurance acts, and agent acted on behalf of applicants and had apparent authority to bind them.[9]

In *New York, Principal Life Ins. Co. v. Locker Group*, 869 F.Supp.2d 359 (2012), the District Court for the Eastern District of New York found that an insured's misrepresentation of his income in a life insurance application supported rescission of the policy, despite the insurer's failure to require third-party verification of the insured's income, the insured's alleged misunderstanding of the income inquiry, and the insurer's delay in seeking rescission, allegedly resulting in ratification; in determining materiality, the relevant inquiry was whether the insurer would have issued the policy had insured truthfully disclosed his income, not whether verification was required, the claim of a misunderstanding lacked any foundation, and the record contained no reasonable indication that the insurer acquiesced in the policy, but rather, it conducted itself in a manner consistent with protecting its right to rescind.

---

[9] . *Those Certain Underwriters at Lloyd's, London Subscribing to Policy No. Buy1780 v. Cleopatra, LLC*, Not Reported in A.3d, 2013 WL 6081460 (N.J.Super.A.D., 2013)

An ERISA administrator was legally correct in determining that participant, who apparently was not legally entitled to be present and work in United States, made material misrepresentation in providing false social security number (SSN) on life insurance enrollment form, and that rescission of policy thus was warranted. Because participant provided false SSN and inhibited administrator's ability to verify his identity, he placed administrator at risk of severe penalties and inhibited its ability to assess underwriting risk, thereby establishing that the misrepresentation was material. [Employee Retirement Income Security Act of 1974, § 2 et seq., 29 U.S.C.A. § 1001 et seq.][10]

In New Jersey, *Henriques v. New Jersey Mfs. Ins. Co.* (Uninsured Motorist Claim) Not Reported in A.2d, 2009 WL 5125021 (N.J.Super.A.D., 2009) held that a misstatement is material if it would have influenced a reasonable insurer's decision in deciding whether to offer insurance at all, in estimating the degree of risk involved, or in setting the rate of the premium. The focus of materiality is at the time the misstatement was made. This rule avoids incentivizing the insurance applicant to gamble that his or her misstatement will turn out to be unimportant. An insured's misstatement is material if when made a reasonable insurer would have considered the misrepresented fact relevant to its concerns and important in determining its course of action.

---

[10] . *Garcia v. American United Life Ins. Co.*, 422 Fed.Appx. 306, 2011 WL 1409222 (C.A.5 (Tex.)), 51 Employee Benefits Cas. 1457 (2011)

In West Virginia, for a misrepresentation in an insurance application to be material, for purposes of the West Virginia statute setting forth grounds for rescission of insurance policy based on misrepresentations, omissions, concealments of facts, and incorrect statements, it must relate to either the acceptance of risk insured or to the hazard assumed by the insurer; materiality is determined by whether the insurer in good faith would either not have issued the policy, or would not have issued a policy in as large an amount, or would not have provided coverage with respect to the hazard resulting in the loss, if the true facts had been made known to the insurer as required by the application for the policy or otherwise. [West's Ann.W.Va.Code, 33–6–7.][11]

Under Pennsylvania law, information provided to obtain insurance is "material," such that misrepresentation of information may justify rescission of policy, if knowledge or ignorance of it would influence decision of issuing insurer to issue policy, or insurer's ability to evaluate degree and character of risk, or determination of premium rate.[12]

In Georgia, unlike California that bases materiality on the underwriter who made the decision to insure, determining whether the false statements made in insurance application were material to the risk assumed by the insurer, as required for rescission of policy, under Georgia law, materiality is evaluated from the perspective of a prudent insurer. [West's Ga.Code Ann. § 33-24-7(b)(2)][13]

---

[11] . *White v. American General Life Ins. Co.*, 651 F.Supp.2d 530 (2009)

[12] . *Radian Ins., Inc. v. Deutsche Bank Nat. Trust Co.*, 638 F.Supp.2d 443 (2009)
[13] . *Medmarc Cas. Ins. Co. v. Reagan Law Group, P.C.*, 525 F.Supp.2d 1334 (2007)

A misrepresentation is material if it naturally and reasonably influences the judgment of the underwriter in making the contract at all, or in estimating the degree or character of the risk, or in fixing the rate of premium. Applying New Jersey law, the District Court for the Southern District of New York reflected that "'[c]ommon sense tells us that an applicant's prior loss history is material to a reasonable insurance company's decision whether to insure that applicant or determination of the premium.'" *Payroll Express*, 216 B.R. at 357 (quoting *Pinette v. Assurance Co. of America*, 52 F.3d 407, 411 (2d Cir.1995)).[14]

---

[14] . *In re Tri-State Armored Services, Inc.*, 332 B.R. 690, Bkrtcy.D.N.J.,2005. (October 03, 2005)

Materiality is determined by considering whether a reasonably careful and intelligent person would have regarded the facts omitted as substantially increasing the chances of the events insured against so as to cause a rejection of the application or different conditions such as higher premiums. [*Ratliff v. Safeway Insurance Co.*, 257 Ill.App.3d 281, 288, 195 Ill.Dec. 473, 628 N.E.2d 937 (1993).] A material misrepresentation may result where an insured fails to disclose material information or provide complete information in response to a question. [*Cohen v. Washington National Insurance Co.*, 175 Ill.App.3d 517, 520, 124 Ill.Dec. 948, 529 N.E.2d 1065 (1988).] "An insurance applicant has the duty to act in good faith, and an insurer is entitled to truthful responses so that it may determine whether the applicant meets its underwriting criteria. Thus, the applicant must disclose all information and let the insurer determine the materiality of the * * * information." [*Garde v. Country Life Insurance Co.*, 147 Ill.App.3d 1023, 1032, 101 Ill.Dec. 120, 498 N.E.2d 302 (1986).] An insurance policy may be voided even if the insured's misrepresentation was a mistake or made in good faith.[15]

---

[15] . *American Service Ins. Co. v. United Auto. Ins. Co.*, 409 Ill.App.3d 27, 947 N.E.2d 382, 349 Ill.Dec. 745 (2011)

## Rescission by Breach of Warranty

Warranties made in insurance policies and applications for insurance are a special type of representation. They are, by definition, material and are usually attached to and form a part of the policy.

In *De Campos v. State Compensation Insurance Fund,* 122 Cal. App. 2d 519, 265 P.2d 617 (Cal.App.Dist.1 01/15/1954) the defendant by its pleadings (1) denied that as between the employer and the carrier the insurance policy was at any time in force in respect to the injury or death of William Ralph Payne, because of asserted misrepresentation and concealment by the employer of material facts with reference to the risk and violation by the employer of specific affirmative warranties as to the person insured, and breach of promissory warranties to report all the employees' earnings and pay premiums thereon; (2) alleged that the employer, having first breached the contract, was in default and could not require the carrier to further perform, nor could the employer recover damages for the alleged subsequent breach by the carrier; (3) alleged and claimed damages from the employer in the amount of compensation which the carrier had paid to the dependents of Payne; and (4) alleged that the employer by its conduct had waived the right, if any it had, to have the proceeding before the Industrial Accident Commission defended by the carrier, and is now estopped to claim any such right.

On December 23, 1940 plaintiffs filed an application for workmen's compensation insurance with the defendant State Compensation Insurance Fund. This application listed only De Campos, Seitzinger, Fleming, and Broyer as copartners doing business under the firm name of Mary Len Mine. In fact, the partnership also included W. R. Payne as general partner. One reason for not listing Payne as a partner was the fact that his credit was not good and it was feared that the defendant would not insure if he were listed as a partner.

Payne was injured July 15, 1941, in the course of his employment, and died as a result of such injury. Not until after this injury did defendant know or have any information tending to indicate that Payne was a member or an employee of the insured partnership. Defendant was induced to issue this policy of insurance to plaintiff by and through the misrepresentation that the four persons named in the policy as the employer were the only members of the copartnership, and the concealment from defendant of the fact that Payne was also a member of the partnership and one of the owners and operators of the business, and plaintiff continued to conceal that fact from defendant until after the death of Payne.

The insurer, although facts existed that supported a rescission, it did not rescind. It resisted Payne's dependents' claims before the Industrial Accident Commission on the basis or theory that Payne was not covered by the policy, not that there was no policy. It lost that contention, was ordered to pay and did pay compensation to those dependents. It seeks to recoup the amount of that payment from the plaintiff-employer as damages proximately caused by the plaintiff-employer's deceit.

The Court of Appeal found that there seems no reasonable doubt concerning the materiality of the misrepresentation, concealment and breach of warranty. "Materiality is to be determined not by the event, but solely by the probable and reasonable influence of the facts upon the party to whom the communication is due, in forming his estimate of the disadvantages of the proposed contract, or in making his inquiries." (Ins. Code, §334.) "An intentional and fraudulent omission, on the part of one insured, to communicate information of matters proving or tending to prove the falsity of a warranty, entitles the insurer to rescind." (Ins. Code, § 338.) "If a representation is false in a material point, whether affirmative or promissory, the injured party is entitled to rescind the contract from the time the representation becomes false." (Ins. Code, § 359.) "The materiality of a representation is determined by the same rule as the materiality of a concealment." (Ins. Code, § 360.) "A statement in a policy of a matter relating to the person or thing insured, or to the risk, as a fact, is an express warranty thereof." (Ins. Code, § 441.) "A warranty may relate to the past, the present, the future, or to any or all of these." (Ins. Code, § 444.) "A statement in a policy, which imports that there is an intention to do or not to do a thing which materially affects the risk, is a warranty that such act or omission will take place." (Ins. Code, § 445.) "The violation of a material warranty or other material provision of a policy, on the part of either party thereto, entitles the other to rescind." (Ins. Code, § 447.)

Therefore, the trial court correctly awarded the defendant reimbursement from plaintiff of the moneys paid to the dependents of Payne pursuant to the final decision of the Industrial Accident Commission.

Plaintiff is confronted with its own warranties including the affirmative warranty that the four persons named as partners were the only members of the insured and that Payne was not a member. Compliance with the terms of this warranty is a condition precedent to a right of recovery insofar as this particular risk is concerned. Noncompliance defeats recovery.

Plaintiff introduced documentary evidence indicating that the insurer did seek to raise these issues, or some of them, before the District Court of Appeal upon review of the commission's decision. That would be too late if timely presentation had not been made to the commission. The absence of reference thereto in the reviewing court's decision suggests that that court so viewed it. This record amply supports the trial court's finding that the decision of the Industrial Accident Commission was not res judicata of the issues of misrepresentation, concealment and breach of warranty.

An insurer tried to bring a case to affirm rescission of a policy of insurance in *Merced County Mutual Fire Insurance Co. v. California*, 233 Cal. App. 3d 765, 284 Cal. Rptr. 680 (Cal.App.Dist.5 08/23/1991) Merced County Mutual Fire Insurance Company (Merced Mutual) appeals from a judgment of dismissal entered after sustaining without leave to amend defendant and respondent State of California's (State) demurrer to the first amended complaint.

In accordance with King's request and in reliance on the representations of the State's agent,

Merced Mutual's agent completed and signed the certificate of insurance provided to King by the State. It is alleged Merced Mutual would not have issued the certificate of insurance but for the representation of the State's agent that the certificate was required as a condition of the lease. In fact, the terms of the lease did not require King to provide such insurance to the State. The statements of the State's representative, Mr. Martin, were false and untrue; Merced Mutual relied upon the statements in issuing the certificate of insurance to the State.

Upon discovering the falsity of the representations of the State's agent, Merced Mutual demanded the State agree to rescind the certificate of insurance, undertake its own defense and reimburse plaintiff for the attorney's fees, costs and expenses plaintiff had incurred or expended in providing a defense to the State. The State refused and insisted it was entitled to coverage as an additional insured under the policy issued to King.

Merced Mutual filed this action to rescind the certificate of insurance attached to the complaint, to declare the State is not an additional insured under the policy issued to King and is not entitled to coverage for the claims arising out of the 1984 traffic accident, and to order the State to reimburse Merced Mutual for its attorney's fees and expenses incurred in defending the State in coordinated action No. 1954.

Civil Code section 1689 provides that a party to a contract may rescind the contract if his consent was given by mistake or fraud exercised by or with the connivance of the party as to whom he rescinds, or of any other party to the contract jointly interested with such party.

An insurance company is entitled to determine for itself what risks it will accept, and therefore to know all the facts relative to the risk insured. It has the unquestioned right to select those whom it will insure and to rely upon him who would be insured for such information as it desires as a basis for its determination to the end that a wise discrimination may be exercised in selecting its risks.

Merced Mutual relies upon its allegation in the complaint that it would not have issued the endorsement but for the representation the lease agreement required the endorsement. Simply stated, it appears the State is saying that Merced Mutual would have issued the certificate whether or not the lease required King to obtain it. Accordingly, we conclude Merced Mutual has or can state a cause of action for rescission.

It was error to have sustained the demurrer without leave to amend on the ground a third party contract was not properly alleged, or the charging allegations against the estate of King were not included or on the ground the allegations of fraud or mistake were not sufficiently specific. Here, Merced Mutual should have been given the opportunity to amend the complaint to correct any defects present.

We are also of the opinion the issues relating to the validity of the endorsement are severable from the main policy and Merced Mutual may seek its rescission without seeking rescission of the main policy.

In Wisconsin, by statute, no failure of a condition prior to a loss and no breach of a promissory warranty constitutes grounds for rescission of an insurance policy unless it exists at the time of the loss and either increases the risk at the time of the loss or contributes to the loss. [Wisconsin Statute § 631.11(3)]

Under the common law, "a breach of a warranty in a policy of insurance voids the policy, without regard to whether the statement warranted relates to a material or an immaterial fact." *First Nat'l Bank v. Nat'l Liberty Ins. Co.*, 194 N.W. 6, 7 (Minn.1923); see *Interstate Indem. Co. v. Ulven*, No. 07–cv–4029, 2009 WL 2208213, at *5–6 (D.Minn. July 22, 2009).

In South Carolina, in *Darwin Nat. Assur. Co. v. Matthews & Megna LLC*, --- F.Supp.2d ----, 2014 WL 3749314 (D.S.C.) Concluded that South Carolina courts do not recognize a distinction between a false warranty and a material misstatement in an application for insurance in terms of the legal standard governing rescission of the insurance policy. *Atl. Life Ins. Co. v. Beckham*, 240 S.C. 450, 458–59, 126 S.E.2d 342, 345 (1962) (citations omitted). Rather, South Carolina law dictates that, regardless of whether a statement is classified as a warranty or a representation, rescission is governed by the same legal standard, and a false statement will not void the policy unless certain elements are proven.[16]

In Illinois, by statute, No misrepresentation or false warranty made by the insured or in his behalf in the negotiation for a policy of insurance, or breach of a condition of such policy shall defeat or avoid the policy or prevent its attaching unless such misrepresentation, false warranty or condition shall have been stated in the policy or endorsement or rider attached thereto, or in the written application therefor. No such misrepresentation or false warranty shall defeat or avoid the policy unless it shall have been made with actual intent to deceive or materially affects either the acceptance of the risk or the hazard assumed by the company. [215 ILCS 5/154.] OneBeacon argues that it is entitled to rescind the Bond because Sykes failed to disclose a "potential claim". The court found a factual dispute and refused to allow summary judgment.[17]

---

[16] . *Carroll v. Jackson Nat'l Life Ins. Co.*, 307 S.C. 267, 268, 414 S.E.2d, 777, 778 (1992).

Rescission of an insurance contract under Utah law is governed by § 31A–21–105 of the Utah Code, which states: "[N]o misrepresentation or breach of an affirmative warranty affects the insurer's obligations under the policy unless: (a) the insurer relies on it and it is either material or is made with intent to deceive; or (b) the fact misrepresented or falsely warranted contributes to the loss."[18]

New York Insurance Law section 3106(a) defines warranty as:

any provision of an insurance contract which has the effect of requiring as a condition precedent of the taking effect of such contract or as a condition precedent of the insurer's liability thereunder, the existence of a fact which tends to diminish, or the non-existence of a fact which tends to increase, the risk of the occurrence of any loss, damage, or injury within the coverage of the contract.

Finding, based upon the statute, that a protective safeguards clause was a warranty rather than a condition precedent, a New York Appellate court refused to grant summary judgment because there was an issue whether the warranty had been complied with at the time of the issuance of the policy even though it was not in effect at the time of loss.[19]

Under Oklahoma law, an insurer may rescind a policy under the following circumstances:

---

[17]. *Federal Deposit Insurance Corporation v. OneBeacon Midwest Insurance Company*, Not Reported in
F.Supp.2d, 2014 WL 1292833 (N.D.Ill., 2014)

[18]. *Colony Nat. Ins. Co. v. Sorenson Medical, Inc.*, Not Reported in F.Supp.2d, 2011 WL 6740537 (E.D.Ky., 2011)

[19]. *Nunez v. U.S. Underwriters Ins. Co.*, 31 Misc.3d 418, 921 N.Y.S.2d 462, 2011 N.Y. Slip Op. 21050 (2011)

All statements and descriptions in any application for an insurance policy or in negotiations therefor, by or in behalf of the insured, shall be deemed to be representations and not warranties. Misrepresentations, omissions, concealment of facts, and incorrect statements shall not prevent a recovery under the policy unless:

1. Fraudulent; or

2. Material either to the acceptance of the risk, or to the hazardassumed by the insurer; or

3. The insurer in good faith would either not have issued thepolicy, or would not have issued a policy in as large an amount, or would not have provided coverage with respect to the hazard resulting in the loss, if the true facts had been made known to the insurer as required either by the application for the policy or otherwise. [36 Okla. Stat. § 3609(A).]

The insurer bears the burden of proof to show not only that the statements were untrue, but also that the misrepresentations were either fraudulent, material to the risks or hazards assumed by the insurer, and, in good faith, the insurer would not have issued the policy, or covered the hazard if the true facts had been known in the application.[20] Oklahoma law requires a finding that the insured intended to deceive the insurer before a misrepresentation or an omission on an insurance application can serve as grounds for nonpayment. Where the evidence is conflicting as to the falsity of insured's statements in the application process, or the intent of the insured, the issues are properly tendered to the jury for resolution.

---

[20] . *Claborn v. Washington National Insurance Co.*, 1996 OK 8, ¶ 7, 910 P.2d 1046, 1049.

In Ohio, the consequences of a misstatement of fact by an insured are entirely different, depending on whether the statement is a warranty or a representation. If the statement is a warranty, a misstatement of fact voids the policy ab initio. However, if the statement is a representation, a misstatement by the insured will render the policy voidable, if it is fraudulently made and the fact is material to the risk, but it does not void the policy ab initio.[21]

An insurer may only rescind or cancel an insurance policy based upon a misrepresentation in Massachusetts, as follows:

"No oral or written misrepresentation or warranty made in the negotiation of a policy of insurance by the insured or in his behalf shall be deemed material or defeat or avoid the policy or prevent its attaching unless such misrepresentation or warranty is made with actual intent to deceive, or unless the matter misrepresented or made a warranty increased the risk of loss." G.L. c. 175, § 186.

Any misrepresentation that results in the insurer's charging a lower premium than it otherwise would have charged is "material."[22] For example, an insured's failure to disclose his second car was material even where it did not technically increase risk of loss as cars were never on the road at the same time. A material misrepresentation in an application for an insurance policy will give the insurer the right to rescind it.

In Utah, no misrepresentation or breach of an affirmative warranty affects the insurer's obligation under the policy unless:

(a)    the insurer relies on it and it is either material or is made withintent to deceive; or

---

[21] . *Allstate Insurance Co. v. Boggs,* 27 Ohio St. 216, 218–219 (1971).

[22] . *Barnstable County Ins. Co. v. Gale*, 425 Mass. 126, 128–129, 680 N.E.2d 42 (1997)

(b)      the fact misrepresented or falsely warranted contributed to theloss. [Utah Code Annotated § 31A–21–105(2)]

The "test for whether a fact is material to the risks assumed under an insurance policy is whether 'reasonable insurers would regard the fact as one which substantially increases the chance that the risk insured against will happen and therefore would reject the application.' "[23]

---

[23] . *ClearOne Communications, Inc. v. Lumbermens Mut. Cas. Co.*, Not Reported in F.Supp.2d, 2005 WL 2716297 (D.Utah, 2005)

## Bad Faith & Punitive Damages

Every lawyer who represents a plaintiff suing an insurance company for the tort of bad faith or the lawyer defending an insurer against claims that it committed the tort of bad faith, must understand, why punitive damages can be awarded to punish an insurer. Through an analysis of punitive damages as applied in the United States to insurance bad faith suits, this book will analyze why the various states allow judges and juries to award punitive damages against insurers in civil litigation.

First and foremost, lawyers and litigants must understand that unlike contract or tort damages punitive damages are awarded to punish the tortfeasor sufficiently to act as a deterrent to others who may be considering to act similarly. Until the 1950's a person suing an insurance company could only recover contract damages. The most the insured could recover, if an insurer breached the contract of insurance, is the benefits promised by the policy. When the courts created the tort of bad faith they changed contract law enormously by allowing unhappy insureds to sue insurers for both contract and tort damages, including punitive damages.

Basic tort damages are designed and expected to provide indemnity to the plaintiff. Tort damages attempt to use money to place the plaintiff in same situation he or she was in before injured by a tortfeasor.

The award of punitive damages provides the plaintiff with sums greater than the damages actually incurred as a result of the tort in a sum sufficient to punish the defendant and deter the defendant – and others – from repeating the wrongful conduct. Punitive damages do not help the insured return to the situation he or she was in before the insurance contract was breached. If they collect the punitive damages the insured is placed in a better position than he or she was in before the breach of the contract.

## Traditional Tort Damages

When an American is damaged by the tortious conduct of another his or her ability to reason analytically disappears. The damaged person becomes angry and wants to punish the person who caused the harm. Indemnity, the general measure of tort or contract damages, is insufficient. The injured person wants revenge, he or she wants the defendant tortfeasor to suffer. The plaintiff is not satisfied with traditional tort damages that merely compensates him or her fairly for the damages incurred.

Punishment was limited to that authorized by statute for criminal conduct of a defendant. The common law of England and the common and statutory law of the United States only allowed tort damages designed to make the plaintiff whole. Damages for breach of contract or for injuries to person or property by the tortious conduct of the defendant were limited to the cost to repair or replace the damaged property or compensate the plaintiff for the injuries incurred. The defendant who acted tortiously - negligent or intentionally - was only required to pay damages resulting from the tortious conduct that placed the plaintiff back in the position he or she was in before the injury or damage.

Civil juries have a difficult enough time establishing appropriate numbers to indemnify a person so that he or she is back the way he or she was before damaged by a tort. To ask a civil jury to, after concluding a tort caused damage to the plaintiff, add to the actual damages an appropriate civil punishment does not appear to be fair to the judge or jury. Punitive damages are assessed by civil juries where only nine out of twelve must agree to punish the defendant. Without the protection given criminal defendants by the Fifth Amendment to the U.S. Constitution and the right to a trial by a jury of the tortfeasors' peers who must vote unanimously to punish the tortfeasor is the reason why punitive damages are controversial.

The wild differences in awards of punitive damages from a single dollar to billions of dollars is evidence of the difficulties the assessment of appropriate quantum of punitive damages give juries. As Benjamin Franklin once said: "Tis more noble to forgive, and more manly to despise, than to revenge an injury." Punitive damages allow revenge and are neither noble nor manly but is a court ordered revenge.

For example, in 2003, according to *"The Blockbuster Punitive Damages Awards"* by W. Kip Viscusi, Cogan Professor of Law and Economics, Harvard Law School, Hauser 302, Cambridge, MA 02138 Published by the Harvard Law School at http://www.law.harvard.edu/programs/olin_center/papers/pdf/473.pdf:

| State | Number of Cases | Punitive Damages |
| --- | --- | --- |
| California | 15 | 39,289,000,000 |
| Texas | 12 | 5,014, 000,000 |
| Alabama | 4 | 4,200,000,000 |
| Illlinois | 4 | 4,025,000,000 |
| Maryland | 4 | 1,072,000,000 |
| Missouri | 3 | 2,220,000,000 |

The courts recognize that punitive damages are private fines levied by civil juries. They are not awarded to compensate for injury. Rather to further the aims of the criminal law to punish reprehensible conduct and to deter its future occurrence. A review of how punitive damages are assessed follows:

**Top 10 California Punitive Damages Verdicts Of 2012:**

1. $125 million against Catholic Healthcare West.
2. $21 million against Jehovah's Witnesses.
3. $20 million against Joe Francis.
4. $18 million against Union Carbide.
5. $15.9 million against UPS, Inc.

6.     $15 million against Donald Sterling.

7.     $10 million against Allstate.

7.     $10 million against Hans Reiser.

9.     $7.7 million against The Price is Right.

10.    $7.5 million against Breg, Inc. and Dr. David Chao.

**Top 10 U.S. Punitive Damages Verdicts Of 2012**

In 2011, none of the top California awards cracked the top 5 nationwide. In 2012, California verdicts show up at #4 and #10 in the top 10 largest awards in the United States according to Horvitz & Levy, LLP at http://www.calpunitives.com/2013/01/the-top-punitive-damages-awards-of-2012.html.

1.     $6 billion (federal district court in New York)

2.     $1.67 billion (federal district court in D.C.)

3.     $236 million (federal district court in D.C.)

4.     $125 million (California)

5.     $100 million (Illinois)

6.     $75 million (Oregon)

7.     $55 million (Florida)

8.     $32 million (Montana)

9.     $25 million (Oregon)

10.    $21 million (California)

"Punitive damages are awarded in the jury's discretion 'to punish [the defendant] for his outrageous conduct and to deter him and others like him from similar conduct in the future.' *Restatement (Second) of Torts* Sec. 908(1) (1979). The focus is on the character of the tortfeasor's conduct – whether it is of the sort that calls for deterrence and punishment over and above that provided by compensatory awards. If it is of such a character, then it is appropriate to allow a jury to assess punitive damages … To put it differently, society has an interest in deterring and punishing all intentional or reckless invasions of the rights of others, even though it sometimes chooses not to impose any liability for lesser degrees of fault." [*Smith v. Wade,* 461 U.S. 30 (1983)]

Punitive damages act as a windfall to the plaintiff's lawyer more than to the plaintiff who was harmed by an insurer's conduct. The plaintiff who is awarded a large punitive damage award is surprised that the operation of federal and state income tax laws, since punitive damages do not indemnify the plaintiff for damages incurred and are, therefore, taxable as income. In fact, since some law firms extract a 50% contingency fee of the punitive damages and take costs and expenses out of the damages awarded before giving any money to the plaintiff, the plaintiff actually receives less than 50% of the total punitive award.

The tax man, however, assesses taxes based on the full award so if the plaintiff receives a $1 million punitive damages award, his lawyer takes $500,000 as his contingency fee and $20,000 in costs and expenses, the plaintiff nets $480,000 of that award. He is then assessed 39% federal taxes – and if he is in a state like California, more than 13% state taxes – the net recovered by the plaintiff will be almost a negative He must pay the federal government $390,000 and the state government $130,000 leaving him only $32,000 net. If expert fees were involved the net recovery disappears quickly. The defendant is punished and the plaintiff's lawyer does very well although he must also pay taxes on his fee. Only the lawyer and the government do well with regard to punitive damages and the plaintiff loses what he or she believed was a windfall.

Precedents are legion with the recognition of the penal nature of punitive damages.[2]

Since the purposes of punitive damages are to punish the defendant and to deter future misconduct by making an example of the defendant it matters not to the court who gets the money and the government does nothing to allow the plaintiff to become rich from a punitive damages award.

Punitive damages – sometimes referred to as exemplary damages – vindictive damages, or smart money will usually exceed actual damages. Punitive damages are not compensatory.

---

[2]      e.g. *Tull v. United States*,481 U.S. 412, 422, and n. 7 (1987); *Memphis Community School District v. Stachura*, 477 U.S. 299, 306, n. 9 (1986); *Silkwood v. Kerr-McGee Corp.*, 464 U.S. 238, 260-261 (1984) (Blackmun, J., dissenting); *Smith v. Wade*, 461 U.S. 30, 59 (1983) (Rehnquist, J., dissenting); *Newport v. Fact Concerts, Inc.*, 453 U.S. 247, 266-267 (1981); *Gertz v. Robert Welch, Inc.*, 418 U.S. 323, 350 (1974); *Rosenbloom v. Metromedia, Inc.*, 403 U.S. 29, 82 (1971) (Marshall, J., dissenting); *Lake Shore & M. S. R. Co. v. Prentice*, 147 U.S. 101, 107 (1893).

Until well into the 19th century, punitive damages frequently operated to compensate for intangible injuries, compensation which was not otherwise available under the narrow conception of compensatory damages. This function reached its peak in the 1960's and 1970's when courts began to allow people to recover tort damages (including punitive damages) for breaches of insurance contracts.

The courts believed it was necessary to create the tort of bad faith as a result of evidence showing abuses by insurers causing damages to those they insured. In so doing, the desire to compensate for intangible injuries as a result of the breach of insurance contracts, never before allowed, the courts claimed that insurers were a special type of contracting party who could be held liable under a new tort called the tort of bad faith. Although the courts did not intend to do so, the tort of bad faith, created a major source of income for lawyers suing and defending insurers. The creation of the new tort increased litigation against insurers as plaintiffs and their lawyers saw the potential of hitting a jackpot with a punitive award.

In *Benavides v. U.S.*, 497 F.3d 526 (5th. Cir., 2007) the Fifth Circuit concluded that 26 U.S.C. § 104(c) does not exclude punitive damages from the gross income of the survivors of a deceased worker when the wrongful death laws of the state in question do not limit recovery to punitive damages

In *Foster v. U.S.,* 249 F.3d 1275 (11th Cir., 2001) and *Stevan v. Commissioner*, 80 T.C.M. 420 (U.S.T.C., 2000) the court concluded that punitive damages must be included as part of the gross income of the plaintiff and is taxable.

**Punitive Damages are Now Ubiquitous**

The law of almost every state, either by statute or court decision, allow the injured person to punish the person who caused the injury and profit from that punishment if the elements or serious wrongful conduct can be proved. The stated purpose for the award of punitive damages is to deter the defendant and others from future wrongful conduct not to allow the plaintiff to profit.

Punitive damages seldom effect the stated purposes, other than punishment, for which they were intended. Rather, in practice their effect is often to punish those who are not parties to the suit.

History has shown that massive punitive damage judgments that make headlines in the press are often reduced, reversed or sent back for retrial. The news of the judgments, however, effect all litigants with similar cases. The press seldom reports with the same vigor, if at all, the reversal of massive punitive damage awards. The damage to the insurance industry or other defendant who is assessed punitive damages, is done by the news of the verdict. Copies of the news stories are immediately delivered to defendants in other cases where punitive damages are sought, with a settlement offer. The insurer is told that a settlement will allow the insurer to avoid similar punishment.

Tort defendants and their Insurers, fearing being painted with the same brush as that of their fellow defendants, no matter how strong their case, will usually settle. The innocent, therefore, pay money they do not owe. The defendant that acted in bad faith does not. It gets a new trial or a severely reduced verdict. Its bad acts, therefore, make it more competitive than the innocent defendant who is wrongly sued and convinced to settle because of the fear of a potential punitive damages award.

The plaintiff who recovers a punitive award is also punished because he pays 40% to 50% of the punitive damages to his or her lawyer on a contingency fee basis and 39% to the U.S. Government of the total award and if he lives in a state like New York or California with more than 10 % to 13 % income tax, the plaintiff will receive almost none of the punitive damages awarded.

## A Method to Defeat Bad Faith Suits

### Excellence in Claims Handling

The best way to defeat a bad faith suit is to avoid the suit altogether. When an insurer and its personnel treat every insurance claim and every insured presenting a claim with excellence in claims handling.

In the last few decades, insurers, in search of profit, have decimated their professional claims staff. They laid off experienced personnel and replaced them with young, untrained, unprepared people. A virtual clerk replaced the old professional claims handler. Process and computers replaced hands-on human skill and judgment. Money was saved by paying lower salaries. Within three months of firing the experienced claims people gross profit increased.

The promises made by an insurance policy are kept by a claims person. Unless the claims person is well-trained, experienced and knowledgeable the ability to keep all of the promises made by an insurance policy cannot be kept. Keeping a professional claims staff dedicated to excellence in claims handling is, in my opinion, cost-effective over long periods of time. A professional and experienced adjuster will save the insurer millions by resolving disputes, paying claims owed promptly and fairly, and by so doing the insurer will avoid breach of contract and bad faith litigation.

The professional claims person is an important part of the insurer's defense against litigation by insureds against insurers for breach of contract and the tort of bad faith. Claims professionals resolve more claims for less money without the need for either party to involve counsel. A happy claimant satisfied with the results of his or her claim will never sue the insurer. An insured who receives everything the policy promised will never sue the insurer for bad faith. An insured whose claim is not covered and has the lack of coverage explained carefully, intelligently, and in language that a lay person would understand, will not sue an insurer for breach of contract or bad faith.

Incompetent or inadequate claims personnel force insureds and claimants to public insurance adjusters and lawyers. Every study performed on claims establishes that claims with an insured or claimant represented by counsel cost more to resolve than those where counsel is not involved. Prompt, effective, professional claims handling saves money for both the insured and the insurer and fulfills the promises made when the insurer sold the policy.

Insurers who believe they can handle first or third-party claims with young, inexpensive, inexperienced and untrained claims handlers should be accosted by angry stockholders whose dividends have plummeted or will plummet as a result. When an insurer compromises on staff, profits, thin as they may have been previously, will move rapidly into negative territory. Tort and punitive damages will deplete reserves. Insurers will quickly question why they are writing insurance. Those who stay in the business of insurance will either adopt a program requiring excellence in claims handling from every member of their claims staff, or they will fail.

Insurance is a business. It must change—this time for the better—if it is to survive. It must rethink the firing of experienced claims staff and reductions in training to save "expense." Insurers should, if they wish to succeed, adopt a program to promote excellence in claims handling that can help insurers keep the promises made by the insurance policy and avoid charges of breach of contract and the tort of bad faith in both first and third-party claims.

Insurers must understand that they cannot adequately fulfill the promises they make to their insureds and their obligations under fair claims practices acts without a professional, well trained and experienced claims staff. An insurer must work vigorously and intelligently to create a professional claims department or recognize it will lose its market and any hope of profit.

Insurance claims professionals should be people who:

- can read and understand the insurance policies issued by the insurer.
- be able to explain the policies issued by the insurer to a lay person in language understandable to anyone with a fourth-grade education.
- understand the promises made by the policy and their obligation, as an insurer's claims staff, to fulfill the promises made.
- are competent and thorough investigators.
- have empathy, and recognize the difference between empathy and sympathy.
- understand medicine relating to traumatic injuries and are sufficiently versed in tort law to deal with lawyers as equals.
- understand how to repair damage to real and personal property and the value of the repairs or the property.
- have available experts who can fulfill knowledge or expertise the claims professional does not have.

An insurer whose claims staff is made up of people who are less than professional will find itself the subject of multiple instances of expensive, counterproductive bad faith litigation. The insurer whose claims staff is made up of insurance claims professionals will find the number of lawsuits against them have dropped logarithmically.

## A Proposal to Create Claims Professionals

To avoid claims of breach of contract, bad faith, punitive damages, unresolved losses, and to make a profit, insurers must maintain a claims staff dedicated to excellence in claims handling. That means they recognize that they are obligated to assist the policyholder and the insurer to fulfill all the promises made by the insurer in the wording of the policy. An insurer can create a claims staff dedicated to excellence in claims handling by, at least:

- Hiring insurance claims professionals.
- If professionals are not available, training all members of the existing claims staff to be insurance claims professionals.
- Training each member of the claims staff annually on the local fair claims settlement practices regulations.
- Supervising each claims handler closely to confirm all claims are handled professionally and in good faith.
- Explaining to each member of the claims staff the meaning of the covenant of good faith and fair dealing.
- Requiring that staff treat every insured with good faith and fair dealing.
- Demanding excellence in claims handling from the claims staff.
- Being ready to dismiss any claims handler who fails to treat every insured with good faith and fair dealing.

If any experienced claims professionals exist on the insurer's staff, the insurer must cherish and nurture them and use their experience and professionalism to train new claims people. If none are available, the insurer has no option but to train its people from scratch using available materials and professionals who have – for a reasonable fee – the ability to properly and effectively train claims personnel.

When the claims staff is made up of claims people who treat all insureds and claimants with good faith and fair dealing and provide excellence in claims handling litigation between the insurer and its insureds will be reduced exponentially.

To keep the professional claims staff operating efficiently and in good faith they must be honored with increases in earnings and perquisites. Conversely, those who do not treat all insureds and claimants with good faith and fair dealing should be counseled and given detailed training. If they continue with less than professional conduct they must be fired. There is no excuse to keep a less than competent, less than professional claims person on staff any more than it is reasonable to keep a pet alligator without a cage.

The insurer must make clear to all employees that it is committed to immediately eliminating staff members who do not provide excellence in claims handling and must be ready to publicly and quickly fire those who do not provide excellence in claims handling.

An excellence in claims handling program can include a series of lectures supported by text materials. It must be supplemented by meetings between supervisors and claims staff on a regular basis to reinforce the information learned in the lectures. To guarantee that the training and requirement for excellence in claims handling is effective he insurer must also institute a regular program of auditing claims files by experienced and professional claims management, to establish compliance with the requirement to deal fairly and in good faith to the insured. The insurer's management must support the training and repeat it regularly and audit claims files to determine the training has taken and is being applied to each claim.

There is no quick and easy solution. The training takes time; learning takes longer. If the insurer does not have the ability to train its staff it should use outside vendors who can do so available from sources like this publication, training from professional organizations, and continuing education providers.

The excellence in claims handling program requires thorough training providing each member of the claims staff with a minimum of the following:

1. How to read and understand the contract that is the basis of every adjustment, including but not limited to:
    a. The formation of the insurance policy.
    b. The need to read every word in the policy as it relates to a claim or potential claim.
    c. The rules of interpretation of insurance contracts applied by the courts.
2. Tort law including negligence, strict liability in tort, and intentional torts.
3. Contract law including the insurance contract, the commercial or residential lease agreement, the bill of lading, nonwaiver agreements, proofs of loss, releases and other claims related contracts.

    a. The duties and obligations of the insured in a personal injury claim.

    b. The duties and obligations of the insurer in a personal injury claim.

    c. The duties and obligations of the insured in a first party property claim.

    d. The duties and obligations of the insurer in a first party property claim.

4. The state's Fair Claims Practices Act and the regulations that enforce it.

5. The thorough investigation:

    a. Basic investigation of an auto accident claim.

    b. Investigation of a construction defect claim.

    c. Investigation of a nonauto negligence claim.

    d. Investigation of a strict liability claim.

    e. Investigation of the first party property claim.

    f. The recorded statement of the first party property claimant.

    g. The recorded statement or interview of a third-party claimant.

    h. The recorded statement of the insured.

    i. The red flags of fraud.

    j. The Special Investigation Unit (SIU) and the obligation of the claims representative when fraud is suspected.

6. Claims report writing.

7. The evaluation and settlement of the personal injury claim.

8. How to retain coverage counsel to aid when a coverage issue is detected.

9. How to control coverage counsel.

10. How to instruct coverage counsel on the issue to be resolved.

11. How to retain defense counsel to defend an insured.

12. Dealing with a plaintiff's lawyer.

13. Dealing with personal injury defense counsel.

14. The evaluation and settlement of the property damage claim.

15. The Appraisal process with regard to first party property claims.

16. Arbitration and mediation and the claims representative.

## Required Continuing Education

State insurance departments across the country are attempting to micromanage the business of insurance with various statutes and regulations. Two such requirements follow. Failure to comply with the continuing education requirements can be used as evidence of an insurer's failure to require its employees to comply with the covenant of good faith and fair dealing. Insurers should not only ensure that their training programs conform to those required by the relevant states, but also that the claims staff consistently apply excellence in claims handling training in compliance with the requirements of the Regulations.

## Continuing Education Requirement

On January 1, 2009, AB 2044—which has been added to the California Insurance Code as § 14090.1—went into effect. Section 14090.1 requires continuing education with the following language:

(a) An individual who holds an insurance adjuster license and who is not exempt under subdivision (b) of this section shall satisfactorily complete a minimum of 24 hours, including ethics, of continuing education courses pertinent to the duties and responsibilities of an insurance adjuster license reported to the insurance commissioner on a biennial basis in conjunction with his or her license renewal cycle.

(b) This section does not apply to either of the following:

(1) A licensee not licensed for one full year prior to the end of the applicable continuing education biennium.

(2) A licensee holding a nonresident insurance adjuster license who has met the continuing education requirements of his or her designated resident state.

Section 15059.1 contains identical provisions that require the same number of continuing education hours for public insurance adjusters, and provides that:

(a) An individual who holds a public insurance adjuster license and who is not exempt under subdivision (b) shall satisfactorily complete a minimum of 24 hours, including ethics, of continuing education courses pertinent to the duties and responsibilities of a public insurance adjuster license, to be reported to the insurance commissioner on a biennial basis in conjunction with his or her license renewal cycle.

(b) This section shall not apply to:

(1) A licensee not licensed for one full year prior to the end of the applicable continuing education biennium.

(2) A licensee holding a nonresident public insurance adjuster license who has met the continuing education requirements of his or her designated state or residence.

In addition, the law authorizes the insurance commissioner to mail an applicant or a licensee a citation and an order assessing a specified fine for a violation the commissioner believes the applicant or licensee committed. Only if the licensee requests a hearing can proceedings be initiated regarding the validity of the citation and order. The issuance of a notice, citation, or order under this provision would not constitute a disciplinary action or an administrative action against the licensee. In essence, the commissioner can punish any licensee without a trial and make the licensee guilty until proven innocent.[20]

**Fraud Training Requirement**

In addition, as of October 7, 2005, California imposed a regulation, at Subchapter 9, Article 2, starting at Section 2698.30 *et seq.*, called the "Special Investigation Unit Regulations."

If you are an employee of an insurer who has any business in California and anything to do with claims or underwriting, an independent adjuster or adjusting firm, a managing general agent, or an appointed agent of any insurer doing business in California and were not trained about insurance fraud recognition by the end of September 2005 you and the insurer are in violation of the California Code of Regulations. The regulations require each insurer to train you annually and to train all new hires within 90 days of hire.

If you and your staff have not been trained by the insurer(s) with whom you are employed or who you represent, and if you do not have a training program in force, you, your employer, and the insurers you represent are in violation of the regulations. Fines of $5,000 to $10,000 can be assessed for each violation.[21] Similar regulations and fines exist in many, if not most, states.

You can protect yourself, and the insurers you represent, from California Department of Insurance audits and fines by complying with these regulations.

The regulations at Section 2698.39 require every admitted insurer to train all "Integral Anti-Fraud Personnel." Very few people employed by an insurer or its agents are not included in this list.

Integral antifraud personnel include:

- claims handlers;
- underwriters;
- agents;
- policy handlers;
- call center staff;
- legal staff; and
- other insurer employees who perform similar duties.

The regulations also require that the admitted insurer maintain:

> [r]ecords of the anti-fraud training provided to all staff [and that they] shall be prepared at the time training is provided and be maintained and available for inspection by the Department on request. The training records shall include the title and date of the anti-fraud training course, name and title and contact information of the instructor(s), description of the course content, length of the training course, and the name and job title(s) of participating personnel.

## Use of The Fair Claims Settlement Practices Regulations in Trial

Regardless of the ruling of Judge Smith dealing with the potential punishments that can be assessed by the CDOI, the Regulations establish the minimum standard of conduct for insurers in California. Insurers who flout the Regulations have no right to gain a competitive edge on insurers who scrupulously follow the Regulations and faithfully discharge their obligations to their insureds. Insurers who follow the law should not be put at competitive disadvantage, particularly at the expense of insureds who may have valid claims.[24] The *Spray* case allowed the insured to assert estoppel because, in violation of the Regulations, the insurer failed to advise its insured, a law firm, of the existence of a private limitation of action or statute of limitations.

The Regulations have made it easier for a litigant to prove an insurer acted in violation of the common law covenant of good faith and fair dealing and committed the tort of bad faith. Similarly, fulfilling the Regulations to the letter can be used by insurers to defend against claims of bad faith. To do so the parties must present evidence concerning the Regulations in a manner that is believable and understandable to a lay jury.

---

[24] . *Spray v. Associated International Insurance Co.,* 71 Cal.App.4th 1260, 84 Cal.Rptr.2d 552, 99 Cal. Daily Op. Serv. 3241 (Cal.App. Dist.2 05/04/1999)

Most litigants present evidence regarding compliance with or failure to comply with the Regulations by use of a claims handling expert. The expert will testify as to his or her conclusion that a party either complied with or failed to comply with the Regulations. A claims handling expert, especially one with an insurer biased history, who testifies that the defendant insurer violated the Regulations can be damning to the defense. Similarly, a claims handling expert who can testify that the insurer fulfilled all of the requirements of the Regulations can convince a jury that it acted in good faith.

For example, during the course of a trial an insurance expert testified as to requirements imposed on insurers under regulations promulgated by the California Department of Insurance. To emphasize the expert's testimony the Regulations were read to the jury by the trial court during the course of the expert's testimony. After all the regulations the expert relied upon had been read by the trial court, the trial court stated:

> Now, by virtue of the fact, ladies and
> gentlemen, that these things call
> themselves standards, you can treat them
> as though they are kind of acknowledged
> standards of behavior in the industry...

The court's instruction, of course, was based upon the expert's testimony and the wording of the Regulation established that the Regulations state a minimum standard for claims handling and failure to fulfill the minimum standard subjects the insurer to punishment by the CDOI. It also allows the jury to conclude that if the evidence established that the insurer failed to fulfill the minimum standards it probably acted in bad faith and was subject to tort damages.

Of course, neither the Insurance Code nor the Regulations adopted under its authority provide a private right of action.[25] Any particular violation of the Regulations does not require a finding of unreasonable conduct.[26] At most the Regulations, when in evidence, may be used by a jury to infer a lack of reasonableness on the part of the insurer. A claims handling expert can, however, convince the jury that it is appropriate for it to infer a lack of reasonableness on the part of the insurer up to and including breach of the covenant of good faith and fair dealing.

Violation of the regulations is not, per se, a breach of contract or an act bad faith rather it is only evidence of a breach or bad faith. Failure to fulfill the minimum standards can be considered by the jury, however, as evidence of bad faith.[27]

An insurance claims handling expert may testify about insurance industry claims settlement practices and refer to the Regulations. The Regulations, by their terms, set forth the minimum standards for claims resolution. A policyholder can use the expert's testimony about violation of the Regulations to support a common law claim of bad faith.[28]

On June 14, 2011, Coast National Insurance Company obtained a unanimous 12-0 jury defense verdict for an insurance company in an insurance bad faith case in San Bernardino, California Superior Court. Your author, Barry Zalma of Zalma Insurance Consultants in Culver City, California, testified as an expert witness on behalf of the insurer.

---

[25] . *Zephyr Park v. Superior Court* (1989) 213 Cal.App.3d 833, 839

[26] . *California Service Station etc. Assn. v. American Home Assurance Co.* (1998) 62 Cal.App.4th 1166, 1175-1176

[27] . *Rattan v. United Services Automobile Association,* 84 Cal.App.4th 715, 84 Cal.App.4th 715, 101 Cal.Rptr.2d 6, 101 Cal.Rptr.2d 6 (Cal.App. 11/01/2000)

[28] . *Jordan v. Allstate Insurance Co.,* 56 Cal.Rptr.3d 312, 148 Cal.App.4th 1062 (Cal.App. Dist.2 03/22/2007)

The case, Joel P. Todd and *Yojana V. Todd v. Coast National Insurance Company, Inc, et al.*, case no. CIVSS 801883, involved the claimed theft of a Chevrolet Trailblazer. The claim was denied by Coast National based on advice of counsel on the grounds that plaintiffs violated the policy's misrepresentation and concealment clause. The car was found after it was reported stolen on the freeway in the direction of the plaintiffs' home with heavy collision damage on the passenger's side, but no parts missing and no evidence of forced entry or ignition tampering. A forensic exam concluded that the car was last driven with a properly cut key. Statements of the plaintiffs' family members differed on key facts, such as what time they were each home before the car was discovered stolen, where the keys were kept, and the activities of the various family members. One of the plaintiffs' family members was an excluded driver on the policy, yet admitted to driving some of the family cars. Plaintiffs argued that the insurer conducted a biased and harassing investigation that focused only on facts that supported denial of the claim, which was unreasonably denied based solely on circumstantial evidence. Complicating matters, plaintiff Joel Todd had just returned from active duty in Iraq, and argued that the handling and denial of the claim severely exacerbated the post-traumatic stress disorder caused by his combat experiences in Iraq.

Mr. Zalma testified that the insurer complied with all of the requirements of the Regulations and that the decision to deny was correct because Coast National followed the custom and practice of automobile material damage insurance practices, completed a thorough and exhaustive investigation, acted in good faith and dealt fairly with the plaintiffs. The jury agreed.

On the other hand a jury found that Lincoln General Insurance Company had acted in bad faith by not shoulder its insured general contractor's liability for bad work in the construction of a home on Laguna Beach's pricey Emerald Bay. In *Hodge v. Lincoln General, 8:08-cv-00288 (C.D. CA, filed March 14, 2008,* Barry Zalma as expert for the plaintiffs Hodge testified that the actions of the insurer violated requirements of the Regulations among other violations of the covenant of good faith and fair dealing. The federal jury took about one and a half hours to decide that Lincoln must pay the Hodges $6 million.

In another case, resolved before trial, a major settlement was reached based on Mr. Zalma's testimony that the Regulations impose on all insurance personnel a detailed laundry list of actions the California Department of Insurance (CDOI) considered wrongful or in violation of the Fair Claims Practices Act, California Insurance Code Section 790.03(h) and established the Regulations as the minimum standards for handling insurance claims in the state.

Mr. Zalma explained that the Regulations impose on all insurance claims personnel the requirement that they read and understand the Regulations or attend an annual training program. They also require that insurers ascertain that every employee involved in any way in the claims process is trained about the Regulations or must swear under oath that he or she has read and understands the Regulations. The defendant had, by its own admission failed to comply with this regulation.

He also testified at deposition that the Regulations require that the insurance claims managing executive attest, under oath, that each employee has been trained annually with regard to and/or understands the Regulations, which the insurer admitted did not exist.

The insurer's actions did not comply with § 2695.5 (h) and § 2695.4 (a) that requires every insurer to disclose all benefits, coverage, time limits or other provisions of any insurance policy issued by that insurer that may apply to the claim presented by the claimant.

The insurer, regularly and with no explanation, violated § 2695.5 (g) that requires response immediately but in no event more than 15 calendar days of communications from Tessera that seeks a response.

The insurer did not, immediately but no later than 15 calendar days after receipt of notice of claim, conduct any "investigation" as defined by the Regulations at § 2695.2(k) as required by § 2695.7(a) and did not inquire into the insured's liabilities, nor did it inquire into the nature and extent of loss or damage claimed by plaintiff whose suit the insured sought defense.

The insurer did not within 40 calendar days after receipt of proof of claim from the insured accept or deny the claim, in whole or in part, and affirm or deny liability as required by § 2695.7(b).

The insurer did not, within 40 calendar days, after receipt of proof of claim give notice of its coverage decision or explain in writing an inability to affirm or deny coverage until it obtains specifically identified needed investigation or documentation in writing as required by § 2695.7(c).

The insurer did not, every 30 days, write to the insured or its counsel to explain the inability to affirm or deny coverage in writing as required by § 2695.7(c).

The insurer did not, immediately but in no event later than 30 calendar days after court established coverage applied, make payment to its insured as required by § 2695.7(h).

Insurers and policyholders should use the availability of the Regulations to provide the jury with sufficient information to determine whether the actions of the insurer were or were not in breach of the covenant of good faith and fair dealing or complied with the insurers obligation to meet the minimum standards of good faith claims handling by complying with or not complying with the minimum standards set by the Regulations.

Although the Regulations were promulgated because there was no direct action available for violation of section 790.03 (h) it has provided a means to prove bad faith better than a direct action that can be damning if presented intelligently and fairly by a well qualified insurance claims expert.

## "Post Loss Underwriting" is an Oxymoron

Some plaintiffs' lawyers contend that rescission is "post loss underwriting" rather than the exercise of a legitimate equitable remedy as old as the common law. They have gone so far as to convince legislatures to place the term "post loss underwriting" in statutes relating to health insurance plans.

Underwriting, by definition, always occurs before the policy comes into being. Those concerned about rescission should not be concerned about "post loss underwriting" but, rather, should be concerned about the abusive use of the rescission remedy by unscrupulous insurers.

Before one can understand the bases for rescission it is necessary to understand the process called underwriting and how insurers select those people or entities the insurer is willing to insure and determine which persons or entities they are not willing to insure.

Post-claim or post-loss underwriting is the alleged practice of an insurer's failure to engage in adequate underwriting until after a claim is submitted and subsequently denying the claim on the basis that the insured is not entitled to the policy.[29]

## What is Insurance Underwriting?

---

[29] . *John Hancock Mut. Life Ins. Co. v. Banerji*, 447 Mass. 875, 858 N.E.2d 277 (2006)

Underwriting is the process of accepting or rejecting risks. It requires a determination of the terms under which the insurance will be written if the risk is acceptable. It is a function unique to the insurance industry. By definition underwriting is a process always performed before a decision is made to insure or not insure and cannot happen after a loss is incurred on the policy.

Modern insurance, when invented in the 18th Century in Lloyd's Coffee Shop on the docks of London, England was a very personal matter. A ship or property owner would discuss with an individual insurer the problems and values which would be involved in a commercial enterprise. They would then agree upon the terms under which the insurer would insure the risk. Together they would draft a contract and the insurer would sign his name at the bottom — he literally underwrote the insurance.

In its original usage, underwriting referred to the operation of the insurance business. In modern usage there is a more restricted meaning applied to the term. Underwriting is a systematic technique for evaluating risks that are offered to an insurer by prospective insureds. The function of underwriting involves evaluating, selecting, classifying, and rating each risk. Underwriting establishes the standards of coverage and amount of protection to be offered to each acceptable risk. It formulates and administers the rules and procedures that are used to ensure that predetermined standards are met by underwriters.

Underwriters are the risk takers, or were hired by the risk takers to act on their behalf. In modern usage in the US underwriting has become more corporate and less individual. Underwriters in the United States are invariably employees of insurance companies and not the actual risk taker who wrote insurance at Lloyd's Coffee Shop. The modern American underwriter performs five basic functions:

1. Selection of risks;

2. Classification and rating of the risk;

3. Policy forms to be used to produce a policy of insurance;

4. Writing a special manuscript policy to meet the individual needs of a unique insured, and

5. Retention and reinsurance.

By performing these five functions, the underwriter increases the possibility of securing a safe and profitable distribution of risks so that the insurer can profit from the insurance risks accepted by the underwriter. As one California court stated:

> An insurance company has the *unquestioned right to select those whom it will insure* and to rely upon him who would be insured for such information as it desires as a basis for its determination *to the end that a wise discrimination may be exercised in selecting its risks.*[30]
> (Emphasis added)

---

[30] . *Robinson v. Occidental Life Ins. Co.* (1955) 131 Cal.App.2d 581, 586.

It is the underwriter who obtains the information necessary to make, and who makes, the decision to select risks the insurer will take. The underwriter expects, based on the information the underwriter receives from the potential insured, that a risk has been agreed that has an opportunity of being profitable. The underwriter, if provided with honest and complete information, is able to wisely discriminate and choose those who can be profitable and refuse those who have a lesser opportunity of being profitable for the insurer.

The remedy of rescission was created by the ecclesiastical courts of ancient England who were charged with reaching fair results rather than a money judgment to make the plaintiff whole. As courts of equity they voided contracts that were obtained by mistake, misrepresentation, concealment or fraud.

Since the turn of the century the plaintiffs' bar has attempted to defeat the remedy of rescission and allow their clients more access to courts of law assessing damages against insurers and avoid equity courts who, if rescission was established, would have no right to damages at law.

In *Nieto v. Blue Shield of California Life & Health Insurance Co.*[31] the California Court of Appeal dealt with one of the first of the so-called "post-loss underwriting" cases and found that plaintiff Julie Nieto failed to disclose information about her medical condition and treatment on a health insurance application she submitted to Blue Shield of California Life & Health Insurance Company (Blue Shield). The court concluded that the application was a "concealment" as defined by California Insurance Code § 331 and a misrepresentation as defined by California Insurance Code § 359. Based on the material misrepresentation and concealment of material fact Blue Shield rescinded the policy it issued to Nieto.

---

[31] . *Nieto v. Blue Shield of California Life & Health Ins. Co.* (2010) 181 Cal.App.4th 60.

In response, Nieto filed an action against
Blue Shield claiming the rescission was
post claim underwriting and an act of bad
faith. The trial court granted Blue Shield's
motion for summary judgment, ruling that
it was entitled to rescission as a matter of
law in view of the undisputed evidence
that Nieto made material
misrepresentations and omissions
regarding her medical history.

The Court of Appeal affirmed the trial court because it
agreed that undisputed evidence established that the
information Nieto provided to Blue Shield was false. The
court, exercising its decision recognized that the covenant
of good faith and fair dealing that applies to all parties to
an insurance contract equally allows an insurer to
reasonably rely upon the statements made by an applicant
on an application for insurance. If the insurer is deceived
by the application it has the right to void the contract and
put the parties back in the position they were in before the
contract was made.

In reaching its conclusion the court noted that in 2005
Blue Shield offered several health insurance plans to
individuals. As part of the determination whether to issue
coverage, Blue Shield provided an application to each
individual seeking coverage that requested detailed
information of past and current health problems, treating
physicians, prescribed medications and recommended
treatment. Using proprietary written guidelines, Blue
Shield evaluated the responses provided by each
applicant to determine eligibility for health insurance and,
if so, at what premium rate.

Blue Shield, like all insurers, relied on the information provided by the applicant when it received the signed application. Blue Shied did not assume the applicant was untruthful nor did it do any investigation to prove she was untruthful at the time it made the decision to insure Nieto. Rather, Blue Shield, believing in and applying the covenant of good faith and fair dealing, only sought to review medical or pharmacy records when the applicant disclosed a condition or treatment that warranted further assessment. When no such condition or treatment was disclosed by the proposed insured, Blue Shield would have no reason to review medical or pharmacy records for the purpose of ascertaining the truthfulness of the applicant's responses.

If the application was incomplete, Blue Shield would contact the applicant to provide additional information. This overall review process is called "underwriting" by the insurance industry.

Nieto, like applicants for almost every type of insurance policy, signed and dated the application directly below the following attestation:

> "I have read the summary of benefits and the terms and conditions of coverage and authorizations set forth above. I understand and agree to each of them. I alone am responsible for the accuracy and completeness of the information provided on this application. I understand that neither I, nor any family members, will be eligible for coverage if any information is false or incomplete. I also understand that if coverage is issued, it may be cancelled or rescinded upon such a finding."

Nieto confirmed in her deposition that she took responsibility for the accuracy and completeness of the information provided in the application. The trial court expressly rejected Nieto's assertion that Blue Shield had engaged in post loss underwriting in violation of a section of the California Insurance Code explaining that before issuing the policy Blue Shield properly completed its underwriting process and resolved all reasonable questions arising from the information provided by Nieto. It further found the evidence showed that Blue Shield was not required to do more, as there was nothing in the application to alert Blue Shield that Nieto's responses were false. The court reasoned that even if Blue Shield had been required to investigate further, there was no evidence to suggest that it would have learned of Nieto's undisclosed condition and treatment.

The undisputed evidence presented to the court established that Nieto made material misrepresentations and omissions on the application regarding her medical condition and treatment. Nieto responded negatively to the inquiries in the "Medical History" portion of the application, when in fact she had suffered from chronic back problems throughout 2005 and previously. Nieto represented that her last doctor's visit had occurred three years earlier, when in fact she had seen and received significant treatment from two doctors regularly and one at least 17 times between February and May 2005, including the day she signed the application. Finally, Nieto represented that she had not taken or been directed to take any prescription medications in the past year, when in fact she had filled at least 10 prescriptions for four different medications and had received two steroid injections as well as an oral steroid.

The undisputed evidence further established that Nieto's misrepresentations and omissions were material. Even if Blue Shield had not pleaded the issue of its insured's fraud as an affirmative defense, the Court in *Cruey v. Gannett Co.* (1998) 64 Cal.App.4th 356, 367 found that an affirmative defense may be raised for the first time in a summary judgment motion absent a showing of prejudice. Addressing the issue of privilege, the Court stated:

> Given the long-standing California court policy of exercising liberality in permitting amendments to pleadings at any stage of the proceedings [citation] and of disregarding errors or defects in pleadings unless substantial rights are affected [citation], we believe that a party should be permitted to introduce the defense of privilege in a summary judgment procedure so long as the opposing party has adequate notice and opportunity to respond.

Because Nieto had sufficient notice of, and an opportunity to respond to, Blue Shield's motion asserting that her fraud justified rescission of the policy, she suffered no prejudice by responding to the motion on the merits. The trial court determined, as a matter of law, that Blue Shield was entitled to rescind coverage if the undisputed evidence showed that Nieto committed fraud by making material misrepresentations or omissions concerning her medical history or condition to Blue Shield before it issued the policy. Turning to the evidence submitted in connection with the motion, the trial court found "that the undisputed facts established each element of fraud and deceit under California law, with respect to [Nieto's] misrepresentations when applying for coverage with Blue Shield Life."

California law permits an insurer to rescind a policy when the insured has misrepresented or concealed material information in connection with obtaining insurance. (*TIG Ins. Co. of Michigan v. Homestore, Inc.* (2006) 137 Cal.App.4th 749, 755-756.) and *Mitchell v. United National Ins. Co.* (2005) 127 Cal.App.4th 457, 468 (Mitchell), among others. The Insurance Code provides, according to *Mitchell*, a "statutory framework that imposes 'heavy burdens of disclosure' 'upon both parties to a contract of insurance, and any material misrepresentation or the failure, whether intentional or unintentional, to provide requested information permits rescission of the policy by the injured party.' [Citation.]" Discussing the purpose of the statutory scheme, the Court stated:

> Requiring full disclosure at the inception of the insurance contract and granting a statutory right to rescind based on concealment or material misrepresentation at that time safeguard the parties' freedom to contract.

Illustrating the application of these provisions, the Court in *Lunardi v. Great-West Life Assurance Co.* (1995) 37 Cal.App.4th 807, affirmed summary judgment in favor of an insurer that rescinded coverage after it discovered the insured had concealed material information about his medical condition during the application process. The insured's obligation to report misstatements in the application is based on the duty of good faith and fair dealing imposed on both parties. The insured's failure to disclose his diagnosis and thereby correct the misstatements in his application constituted a breach of the continuing duty and provided a basis for rescission.

California, by statute and precedent allows courts to confirm rescission of an insurance policy based on an insured's negligent or inadvertent failure to disclose a material fact in the application for insurance.[32]

---

[32] . *Imperial Casualty & Indemnity Co. v. Sogomonian* (1988) 198 Cal.App.3d 169

Nieto relied on the appellate court decision called *Hailey v. California Physicians' Service* (2007) 158 Cal.App.4th 452 (Hailey). She contended, unsuccessfully, that there were triable issues of fact as to whether Blue Shield reasonably completed the medical underwriting process in this case. The Court of Appeal concluded that *Hailey* is both legally and factually inapposite and agreed with the trial court that the undisputed evidence showed that Blue Shield conducted a reasonable investigation and its rescission was not due to any failure to resolve reasonable questions arising from the application. In simple language you cannot lie on an application and then complain that the insurance company did not catch the lies when they were made.

Hailey involved an interpretation of Health and Safety Code section 1389.3, which applies exclusively to health care service plans licensed and regulated by the Department of Managed Health Care. In *Hailey*, the insured completed a Blue Shield application, where Mrs. Hailey claimed she mistakenly believed the application sought information only about her – not her husband and son for whom she also sought coverage; she also claimed that she incorrectly underestimated her husband's weight.

After Blue Shield extended coverage to the insured and her family, the insured's husband was admitted to the hospital for stomach problems and later became completely disabled as the result of an automobile accident. Following the first hospitalization, a Blue Shield investigation revealed that the insured had misrepresented and omitted material information concerning her husband's medical condition.

Blue Shield rescinded the policy. The trial court granted summary judgment in favor of Blue Shield on the insured's complaint for breach of contract and breach of the implied covenant of good faith and fair dealing and on Blue Shield's declaratory relief cross-complaint. The Hailey appellate court reversed, concluding that there were triable issues of fact as to whether Blue Shield engaged in post claims underwriting and whether the insured willfully misrepresented her husband's medical condition.

When the *Hailey* case, on remand, went to trial the Haileys' admitted that they intentionally misrepresented material facts to Blue Shield. Their suit was summarily dismissed mid-trial thereby putting a stake through the heart of the Haileys' post loss underwriting allegation. Blue Shield was required to try the case twice and take it through the litigation and appellate process just to have the Haileys' admit that they obtained the insurance by fraud.

Rescission, as the Court of Appeal found in *Nieto*, has nothing to do with claims.

Underwriting is a decision making process based upon information submitted to the insurer by the proposed insured to convince the insurer to take a risk and insure the proposed insured. When, as did the Haileys and Nieto, the proposed insured lies to obtain the insurance the insurer may seek equity from the court and have the contract voided. To do otherwise would be unfair and allow a fraud to profit from wrongful conduct.

Rescission is an important equitable remedy hoary with age. It should not be limited by claims of bad faith claims handling. Once an insurer learns it was deceived into insuring someone it would not have insured, whether before or after the insurer was sued, it is still entitled to legitimately exercise the right to rescind. It was for that reason that the California Legislature provided both parties to an insurance contract by the California Insurance Code the right to declare a policy void and make both parties whole as if there was never a contract of insurance.

As a general proposition, federal courts sitting in diversity have authority to decide state law claims seeking rescission of an insurance policy.[33]

The California Court of Appeal, the Ninth Circuit Court of Appeal and the California Supreme Court continue to enforce the right and warn those who would attempt to deceive an insurer that they will receive nothing from their deception and find that they may receive no benefit from a legitimate claim that would have been paid if there was no deception.

In *Lewis v. Equity Nat'l Life Ins. Co.*, 637 So.2d 183, 185–86 (Miss.1994) the Mississippi Supreme Court found merit in the plaintiff-insured's claims that the insurer engaged in post-claim underwriting and that the insurer's agent misrepresented information in a policy application. The Court found no evidence of any similar "extreme factual situations" presented by the Plaintiffs in the case. Post-claim underwriting occurs when "an insurer, rather than refusing to write a policy, will wait until after a claim is filed to deny coverage on grounds that the policy should not have been written in the first place." *Dixie Ins. Co. v. Mooneyhan*, 684 So.2d 574, 589 (Miss.1996) (McRae, J., dissenting). The Mississippi Supreme Court has held:

---

[33] . See, e.g., *C.N.R. Atkin v. Smith*, 137 F.3d 1169, 1172 (9th Cir. 1998); *Gasaway v. Nw. Mut. Life Ins. Co.*, 26 F.3d 957, 958 (9th Cir. 1994).

> An insurer has the obligation to its
> insureds to do its underwriting at the time
> a policy application is made, not after a
> claim is filed. It is patently unfair for a
> claimant to obtain a policy, pay his
> premiums and operate under the
> assumption that he is insured against a
> specified risk, only to learn after he
> submits a claim that he is not insured, and,
> therefore, cannot obtain any other policy
> to cover his loss. The insurer controls
> when underwriting occurs. It therefore
> should be estopped from determining
> whether to accept an insured six months
> or more after a policy is issued. If the
> insured is not an acceptable risk, the
> application should [be] denied up front,
> not after a policy is issued. This allows the
> proposed insured to seek other coverage
> with another company since no company
> will insure an individual who has suffered
> serious illness or injury.

As logical as is the analysis of the Mississippi Supreme
Court it does not take into consideration the fact that
people lie to their insurance companies to obtain
insurance. If the lie is not obvious an application
revealing an excellent risk may be a total fraud. In such
a case the lie is usually never discovered until a claim is
made. Post loss underwriting should, in logic, only be
applied if the insurer knew the truth at the time the
application was submitted and did not exercise the right
to refuse the risk. As a result, in *Eagle Transp., LLC v.
Scott,* F.Supp.2d, 2012 WL 1712352, (SD Miss., 2012)
concluded that since the insurer asked for the
information it needed and since the insured provided
false answers to the insurer it did not engage in post-
claim underwriting and the insured the policy was
properly rescinded.

Illinois law has no prohibition on post-claim underwriting. However, while an insurance company might have no duty to conduct an investigation into the truthfulness of an applicant's answer, if it wishes to rescind certain types of policies based on a misrepresentation in the application for that policy, the plain language of Illinois statutes[34] limits the amount of time in which it can do so.

Refusing to apply a post-claim underwriting argument the District Court for the Southern District of West Virginia held that the insurer, MassMutual, put Billy Jordan and Defendant on notice that a material misrepresentation could result in the Policy being rescinded and that there was a two year period after which the policy is incontestable. Further, this notice was provided both when Billy Jordan was applying for the Policy, and in the Policy itself. The insurer was granted summary judgment on its claim of rescission.[35]

In *Harper v. Fidelity and Guar. Life Ins. Co.*, 234 P.3d 1211, 2010 WY 89 (Wyo 2010) the Wyoming Supreme Court rejected claims of post-claim underwriting and affirmed the rescission of an insurance policy because Mr. Harper's application contained omissions and misrepresentations, and summary judgment is appropriate where the misrepresentation is of such a nature that there can be no dispute as to its materiality. Such was the case in this instance. Furthermore, the Wyoming Supreme Court concluded that an insurer is under no duty to investigate the truthfulness of an applicant's responses unless it has notice that those responses might not be truthful or accurate.

---

[34] . *Standard Mut. Ins. Co. v. Jones*, 2012 IL App (4th) 110526, 965 N.E.2d 1129, 358 Ill.Dec. 650

[35] . *Massachusetts Mut. Life Ins. Co. v. Jordan*, Not Reported in F.Supp.2d, 2011 WL 1770435 (S.D.W.Va.)

The Third Circuit Court of Appeal noted that the concept of "post-claim underwriting" itself is nebulous, particularly because it is difficult to draw a distinction between post-claim eligibility investigation and post-claim underwriting. For example, Pennsylvania law provides that it is not bad faith to conduct a thorough investigation into a questionable claim. The insured's concept of "post-claim underwriting" would usurp this general principal and prevent insurers from engaging in post-claim investigations, even in the face of incontrovertible evidence that an insured made a clear misrepresentation.[36] The Third Circuit, so finding, recognized that claims of post-claim underwriting as a method of preventing an insurer from rescinding a policy, was an invitation to fraud and deprived the insurer of the fairness essential to a claim of rescission.

In *Hornback v. Bankers Life Ins. Co.*, 176 S.W.3d 699 Ky App, 2005, the Kentucky court of appeal concluded that an insurance company that issues a policy based on the applicant's answers, without any investigation, is not precluded from raising the defense of fraud or material misrepresentation after a claim is submitted. (*State Farm Mut. Auto. Ins. Co. v. Crouch*, 706 S.W.2d 203, 206 (Ky.App.1986)). When an insured misrepresents material facts on the application, the insurer is justified in denying coverage and rescinding the policy immediately upon discovering that it had been deceived. In so finding the Court of Appeal refused to consider claims of post-claim underwriting and affirmed the rescission.

---

[36] . *Northwestern Mut. Life Ins. Co. v. Babayan*, 430 F.3d 121 (CA 3 (PA) 2005)

Claims of post-claim or post-loss underwriting should be looked at with a great deal of skepticism. As the *Hailey* case made clear even when rescission was refused and the case was sent back to the trial court for trial, the Hailey's, on cross-examination, admitted that they intentionally misrepresented their health conditions when applying for the insurance. Their suit was immediately dismissed for fraud in the inception and they were lucky that they were not prosecuted for attempted insurance fraud. They clearly cost their putative insurer a great deal of money defending through trial, an appeal and a second trial, only to admit fraud. They hoped, by claiming the tort of bad faith, to bludgeon the insurer into a settlement for fear of a bad faith judgment with punitive and tort damages available in addition to the benefits promised by the policy.

The theory of post-claim underwriting sounds fair, on its face, sufficient to cause some states to enact legislation prohibiting it. Once the theory is taken to its logical ending it is really a method to assist unscrupulous insureds to defraud their insurer. For example if proposed insured, suffering from Ebola, applies for insurance and claims perfect health, and received a life insurance policy based on the application, should not be able to claim that the insurer when it rescinds the policy after the Ebola victims death, to be refused rescission because it is applying post-claim underwriting. What it is actually doing is is seeking fairness from a court to prevent it from honoring a fraud.

## The Law of Unintended Consequences

The law of unintended consequences is not statutory. No state or federal government has enacted it into law. No executive has signed the law. It is, rather, a law of the nature of people. It is an adage or idiomatic warning that an intervention in a complex system always creates unanticipated and often undesirable outcomes.

Science and general observation allows the statement that actions of people, especially of governments, will always have effects that are unanticipated or unintended. Economists and other social scientists have heeded its power for centuries. Regardless, for just as long, politicians, insurers and popular opinion have largely ignored it to their detriment.

## PHILOSOPHERS, ECONOMISTS AND POLITICIANS

The concept of unintended consequences is one of the building blocks of economics. Adam Smith's "invisible hand," the most famous metaphor in social science, is an example of a positive unintended consequence. Smith maintained that each individual, seeking only his own gain, "is led by an invisible hand to promote an end which was no part of his intention," that end being the public interest. "It is not from the benevolence of the butcher, or the baker, that we expect our dinner," Smith wrote, "but from regard to their own self-interest."

Most often, however, the law of unintended consequences illuminates the perverse unanticipated effects of legislation and regulation. In 1692 the English philosopher John Locke, a forerunner of modern economists, urged the defeat of a parliamentary bill designed to cut the maximum permissible rate of interest from 6 percent to 4 percent.

Locke argued that instead of benefiting borrowers, as intended, it would hurt them. People would find ways to circumvent the law, with the costs of circumvention borne by borrowers. To the extent the law was obeyed, Locke concluded, the chief results would be less available credit and a redistribution of income away from "widows, orphans and all those who have their estates in money."

In the first half of the nineteenth century, the famous French economic journalist Frédéric Bastiat often distinguished in his writing between the "seen" and the "unseen." The seen were the obvious visible consequences of an action or policy. The unseen were the less obvious, and often unintended, consequences. In his famous essay "What Is Seen and What Is Not Seen," Bastiat wrote: "There is only one difference between a bad economist and a good one: the bad economist confines himself to the visible effect; the good economist takes into account both the effect that can be seen and those effects that must be foreseen." [Online at: http://www.econlib.org/library/Bastiat/basEss1.html]

Bastiat applied his analysis to a wide range of issues, including trade barriers, taxes, and government spending.

The law of unintended consequences provides the basis for many criticisms of government programs. Unintended consequences can add so much to the costs of some programs that they make the programs unwise even if they achieve their stated goals. For instance, the U.S. government has imposed quotas on imports of steel in order to protect steel companies and steelworkers from lower-priced competition. The quotas do help steel companies. But they also make less of the cheap steel available to U.S. automakers. As a result, the automakers have to pay more for steel than their foreign competitors do. So, a policy that protects one industry from foreign competition makes it harder for another industry to compete with imports.

Similarly, Social Security has helped alleviate poverty among senior citizens and the disabled. Many economists argue, however, that it has carried a cost that goes beyond the payroll taxes levied on workers and employers. Martin Feldstein, and others, maintain that today's workers save less for their old age because they know they will receive Social Security checks when they retire. If Feldstein and the others are correct, it means that less savings are available, less investment takes place, and the economy and wages grow more slowly than they would without Social Security.

The law of unintended consequences is at work always and everywhere. People outraged about high prices of plywood in areas devastated by hurricanes, for example, may advocate price controls to keep the prices closer to usual levels. An unintended consequence is that suppliers of plywood from outside the region, who would have been willing to supply plywood quickly at the higher market price, are less willing to do so at the government-controlled price. Thus results a shortage of a good where it is badly needed.

Government licensing of electricians, to take another example, keeps the supply of electricians below what it would otherwise be, and thus keeps the price of electricians' services higher than otherwise. One unintended consequence is that people sometimes do their own electrical work, and, occasionally, one of these amateurs is electrocuted.

If a firm offers complete insurance for bike theft it may distort consumer behavior and reduce the incentive for consumers to lock a bike. This is why insurance companies usually insist on a premium – making sure consumers still have an incentive to look after their bike.

Insurance is controlled by the courts, through appellate decisions, and by governmental agencies, through statute and regulation. Compliance with the appellate decisions, statutes, and regulations—different in the various states—is exceedingly difficult and expensive.

In the United States alone, people pay insurers more than $1.2 trillion in premiums, and insurers pay out in claims and expenses as much or more than they take in. Profit margins are small because competition is fierce, and a year's profits can be lost to a single firestorm, hurricane, or flood.

The business of insurance is, unfortunately, subject to the law of unintended consequences as if it were on steroids.

## INSURANCE AS A NECESSITY

Neither the courts nor the governmental agencies seem to be aware that in a modern, capitalistic society, insurance is a necessity. No prudent person would take the risk of starting a business, buying a home, or driving a car without insurance. The risk of losing everything would be too great. By using insurance to spread the risk, taking the risk to start a business, buy a home, or drive a car becomes possible.

Insurance has existed since a group of Sumerian farmers, more than 5,000 years ago, scratched an agreement on a clay tablet that if one of their number lost his crop to storms, the others would pay part of their earnings to the one damaged. Over the eons, insurance has become more sophisticated, but the deal is essentially the same. An insurer, whether an individual or a corporate entity, takes contributions (premiums) from many and holds the money to pay those few who lose their property from some calamity, like fire. The agreement, a written contract to pay indemnity to another in case a certain problem, calamity, or damage occurs by accident, is called insurance.

In a modern industrial society, almost everyone is involved in or with the business of insurance. They insure against the risk of becoming ill, losing a car in an accident, losing business due to fire, becoming disabled, losing their life, losing a home due to flood or earthquake, or being sued for accidentally causing injury to another. They are insurers, insureds, or people dependent on one another.

## SOME EXAMPLES OF UNINTENDED CONSEQUENCES & INSURANCE

Simplified Wording Causes Ambiguity

Insurance contracts can be simple or exceedingly complex, depending on the risks taken on by the insurer. Regardless, insurance is neither more nor less than a contract whose terms are agreed to by the parties to the contract. Over the last few centuries, almost every word and phrase used in insurance contracts have been interpreted and applied by one court or another. Ambiguity in contract language became certain. However, the average person saw the insurance contract as incomprehensible and impossible to understand.

Courts, struggling to understand policies of insurance added to the concern of Legislators:

> As said in Insurance Company of *North America v. Electronic Purification Company*, 67 Cal. 2d 679, 689, 63 Cal. Rptr. 382, 433 (1967), the insurance company gave the insured coverage in relatively simple language easily understood by the common man in the marketplace, but attempted to take away a portion of this same coverage in paragraphs and language which even a lawyer, be he from Philadelphia or Bungy, would find difficult to comprehend. [*Hays v. Pacific Indemnity Group,8* Cal. App. 3d. 158, 80 Cal. Rptr. 815 (1970).]

Ostensibly to protect the public, to salve the concerns of jurists like the one quoted above, insurance regulators and Legislatures decided to require that insurers write their policies in "easy to read" language. Because they were required to do so by law, the insurers changed the words in their contracts into language that people with a fourth-grade education could understand. Precise language interpreted by hundreds of years of court decisions was disposed of and replaced with imprecise, easy to read language. For examples of the "easy to read" or "plain English statutes" go to Appendix 1.

The law of unintended consequences came into play. Instead of protecting the consumer, the imprecise language resulted in thousands of lawsuits determined to impose penalties on insurers for attempting to enforce ambiguous "easy to read" language. The lawsuits cost insurers and their insureds millions of dollars to get court opinions that interpret the language and reword their "easy to read" policies to comply with the court decisions. For more than 30 years, the unintended consequence of a law designed to avoid litigation has done exactly the opposite.

The attempts by the regulators and courts to control insurers and protect consumers were made with the best of intentions. The judges and regulators found it necessary to protect the innocent against what they perceived to be the rich and powerful insurer. Unfortunately, the plain English statutes had the opposite effect. But, of course, the fact that easy to read policies cause more problems than they cure, the laws and regulations have not been changed.

**Bad Faith Causes Bad Behavior**

In the 1950s, the California Supreme Court created a tort new to U.S. jurisprudence: the tort of bad faith.

A tort is a civil wrong from which one person can receive damages from another for multiple injuries. The tort of bad faith was created because an insurer failed to treat an insured fairly, and the court felt that the traditional contract damages were insufficient to properly compensate the insured. The court allowed the insured to receive, in addition to the contract damages that the insured was entitled to receive under the contract had the insurer treated the insured fairly, damages for emotional distress and punitive damages to punish the insurer for its wrongful acts. Insureds, lawyers for insureds, regulators, and courts across the United States cheered the action of the California Supreme Court, for providing a fair remedy to abused insureds. Most of the states adopted the tort created by the California Supreme Court either by statute or court decision.

After the creation of the tort of bad faith, if an insurer and insured disagreed on the application of the policy to the factual situation, damages were no longer limited to contract damages as in other commercial relationships. If the court found that the insurer was wrong, it could be required to pay the contract amount and damages for emotional distress, pain, suffering, punishment damages, attorney fees, and any other damages the insured and the court could conceive in order to deter other insurers from treating their insureds badly.

The courts and legislators adopting the tort of bad faith hoped that the tort of bad faith would have a salutary effect on the insurance industry and force insurers to treat their insureds fairly. However, claims for $40 wrongfully denied resulted in $5 million verdicts. Juries, unaware of the reason for and operation of insurance, decided that insurers that did not pay claims were evil and that they wrote contracts so they never had to pay. The jurors were convinced it was appropriate to punish insurers severely even when the insurer's conduct was correct and proper under the terms of its contract.

The massive judgments were publicized, and many insurers decided fighting their insureds in court was too expensive regardless of how correct their position was on the contract. They found it less expensive to pay than to fight just as shop owners threatened by the Mafia decided it was better to pay protection to the Mob rather than fight.

Most of the massive verdicts were reversed or reduced on appeal. The bad actors raised their premiums and lost little business. Other insurers, faced with the massive verdicts, allowed fear to control reason, and paid claims that were improper or fraudulent. The extra cost was passed on to all insurance consumers. The insurers who acted improperly were punished less than then honest insurers who were threatened with punitive damages. The insurers who treated their insureds badly, in fact, profited since they continued their wrongful acts and only were required to pay the few insureds that sued. Those that did not sue added to the wrongdoers' profit margins. Honest insurers paid frauds and claims they did not owe and found they needed to raise premium charges to cover the extra expense. The increased premium paid by insureds to cover the extra expense were a clear example of the effect of the law of unintended consequences.

The law of unintended consequences struck the insurance industry and the insurance buying public. Rather than deter wrongful actions the law of unintended consequences resulted in punishing the honest and correct insurers, honoring the insurers who acted in bad faith with profit, and allowed many frauds to succeed.

**Obamacare**

The Patient Protection and Affordable Care Act (PPACA) also known as Obamacare is a good example of good intentions being defeated by the law of unintended consequences.

The primary aim of the law was to boost the number of Americans covered by "high quality" health insurance and protect those Americans who could not afford health insurance. Achieving that objective meant getting a greater fraction of small companies to provide such plans. While more than 98 percent of businesses with 200 or more employees offered employee health insurance, the figure dropped to 61 percent of companies with fewer than 200 employees, according to a report by the Kaiser Family Foundation.

The government's plan combined carrots and sticks. The carrots included new insurance marketplaces where small businesses could buy health insurance cheaper, combined with tax credits to help them provide coverage for low-wage employees. The stick? Businesses with more than 49 workers would have to pay a fine if they didn't offer full-time employees the option of minimum coverage.

Policy makers expected that small businesses without health benefits before the passage of the PPACA would start providing insurance to their employees, while those already offering insurance, would maintain it. Unfortunately, the law of unintended consequences intervened.

To avoid penalties, small-business owners cut back on hiring so they never had 49 full time employees. Business owners also cut employees' hours. Because they faced a fine if they failed to offer health insurance to "full-time" employees, one solution for some companies was to turn employees into part-timers. A Gallup survey revealed that 18 percent of small-business owners have responded to the PPACA by reducing employee work-hours.

Small business owners did not respond enthusiastically to the tax credit carrot the way lawmakers had hoped either. Before the law passed, the White House estimated 4 million small businesses would be eligible for the Health Care Tax Credit if they provided employee health insurance. However, in 2011, only 360,000 actually applied for it. The credit wasn't rich enough to motivate business owners to take it and for many, the process was too cumbersome to be worthwhile.

The law did little to curb the rise in the cost of employee health insurance, as many supporters had hoped. The average premium for family coverage rose logarithmically. Fewer business owners provided insurance if they are unable to afford the required insurance policies.

If policy makers want entrepreneurs to provide high quality health insurance to employees, they need to better align their objectives with small-business owners' goals. If not, lawmakers will simply keep undermining their own efforts.

Similar effects resulted in the individual health insurance markets where thousands of individuals decided it was better to pay the fine rather than pay the egregious premiums for health insurance with unreasonably high deductibles.

## BAD FAITH SET-UPS

Bad faith insurance claims are successful when a plaintiff can prove that the insurance company wrongfully denied an insurance claim and deprived the insured of the benefits of the contract of insurance without good cause. Bad faith insurance suits can arise in the context of any insurance policy. California created the tort of bad faith by court decision. Florida, on the other hand, like many states created by legislation liability for insurers who act in bad faith in denying insurance claims. Since most states allow suit for the tort of bad faith it often seems that every claim that is rejected – whether correctly or wrongfully – results in a suit alleging breach of contract and the tort of bad faith.

In light of the substantial damage awards attendant to bad faith claims, plaintiffs' attorneys have great incentive to try to maneuver insurance companies into committing acts that may constitute bad faith. They may, and fairly often do, attempt such "set-ups" by creating a situation where the insurer refuses to settle a tort claim within policy limits within a limited period of time. The plaintiff's purpose, of course, is to recover substantial extra-contractual damages, including attorneys' fees, where permitted. In short, since a bad faith verdict can be vastly more lucrative than simply collecting on a "within policy limits" claim, the temptation for a lawyer to take advantage of a young, inexperienced or inadequate insurance adjuster, overcomes any sense of morality or the need to obtain a settlement that is in the best interests of the lawyers' clients.

With bad faith claims viewed as the gateway to recovering attorney fees and damages well in excess of policy limits, insurers and policyholders counsel need to be well versed in addressing scenarios in which an insurer's allegedly flawed investigation, settlement practices, and/or noncompliance with statutory claims handling requirements open the door to extracontractual disputes.

While bad faith claims start with establishing some form of unreasonable conduct by the insurer, something more than negligence, a mistake, or poor judgment is required to present a meritorious bad faith claim. This holds true whether the bad faith claim rests on the insurer's alleged breach of the implied covenant of good faith and fair dealing, its fiduciary or quasi-fiduciary obligations owed to its insured, or its violation of unfair insurance practices or claims handling statutes.

Some fact situations that can easily result in a bad faith suit include:

- ❖ Low policy limit and high exposure claims;
- ❖ Lost opportunities to settle within limits;
- ❖ Failure to apprise insured of material litigation or settlement developments;
- ❖ Flawed investigation unduly focused on developing grounds to deny claim;
- ❖ Competing claims for policy limits;
- ❖ Mishandled control of defense, including disregard of conflicting interests and/or insured's entitlement to independent counsel;
- ❖ Failing to timely apprise insured of coverage limitations;
- ❖ Overlooked traps in demand letters and/or insufficient attention to efforts to establish bad faith claim in problematic jurisdictions;

❖ Material violation of statutory claims handling requirements; and/or

❖ Problematic claims file entries.

As a result, the bad faith set-up became common. The bad-faith set-up is not a new tactic. In 1985, Justice Kaus of the California Supreme Court observed:

> "It seems to me that attorneys who handle policy claims against insurance companies are no longer interested in collecting on those claims, but spend their wits and energies trying to maneuver the insurers into committing acts which the insured can later trot out as bad faith." *White v. W. Title Ins. Co.*, 710 P.2d 309, 328 n.2 (Cal. 1985) (Kaus, J., concurring and dissenting).

In *J.B. Aguerre, Inc. v. American Guarantee & Liability Ins. Co.* (1997) 59 Cal.App.4th 6, 68 Cal.Rptr.2d 837, the Court of Appeal affirmed a judgment of dismissal on demurrer, holding a liability insurer did not act unreasonably as matter of law in refusing to meet the plaintiff's $2 million settlement demand, despite the alleged risk of exposing the insured to uncovered punitive liability. The insured's alleged fear of his punitive exposure coerced him to contribute to a settlement out of duress. Justice Neal observed as follows:

"What we have here, at bottom, is an effort by [the insured] to concoct a bad faith claim out of whole cloth with the 'ingenious assistance of counsel.' [The insured] has attempted to position itself to pursue a high stakes, bad faith case, seeking punitive damages, from which it hopes to emerge not only with the [underlying] claim disposed of at no cost to [the insured], but a profit as well in the form of damages recovered from [the insurer]. [¶] Bad faith litigation is not a game, where insureds are free to manufacture claims for recovery. Every judgment against an insurer potentially increases the amounts that other citizens must pay for their insurance premiums."
Id. at pp. 17-18, 68 Cal.Rptr.2d 837.)

Bad faith set-ups most frequently originate in the third-party context. When an insurer is defending an insured against a tort claim and there are insufficient limits available to compensate the insured party. In this context, the set-up involves attempts to cause an insurance company to reject a policy limits settlement offer. Third-party claimants and their counsel have come up with various ways in which to present their offers to reduce the chance that the insurer will actually accept the offer within the stated time period.

The plaintiff's goal, of course, is to obtain a sizeable excess verdict. If successful, the next step in the strategy is for claimant's counsel to enter into an agreement with the insured whereby claimant gives a covenant not to execute on the judgment in exchange for an assignment of the claim based on bad faith failure to settle. The most common form of a bad faith set-up is to make a settlement demand – typically policy limits – with an unreasonable time demand.

A claimant may make a settlement demand with an unrealistic time limitation before the insurance company has full access to the information bearing on liability and damages. The insurance company often declines to meet the demand, explaining that it needs further information. This position is then portrayed as a failure to settle, and will then be used against the insurance company as evidence of unreasonable conduct in the settlement of the case

As one firm put it: "A bad faith case is a plaintiff's attorney's dream. Every insurance cliché, big business prejudice and 'underdog' sentiment, can and should be used. Irrespective of the merits of the defense, insurers are target defendants." [Timothy W. Monsees, *Trial Strategy—The Insurance Bad Faith Case*, Monsees & Mayer P.C., www.monseesmayer.com/Articles/TrialStrategy-The-Insurance-Bad-Faith-Case.shtml (last visited June 22, 2016).] These developments have resulted in the bad faith landscape in some jurisdictions appearing geared more closely to providing policyholder counsel with a lucrative recovery than safeguarding the appropriate balance of interests between insurer and insured.

With bad faith claims viewed as the gateway to recovering attorney fees and damages well in excess of policy limits, insurers and policyholders counsel need to be well versed in addressing scenarios in which an insurer's allegedly flawed investigation, settlement practices, and/or noncompliance with statutory claims handling requirements open the door to extracontractual disputes.

When courts and juries see through this conduct as a set-up – as an orchestrated plan by the claimant or her counsel – they are more hesitant to find the insurance company liable for bad faith. Unfortunately, more often than not, neither the court nor the jury seeks through the conduct as a set-up and allow prejudice against insurers to carry the day and a punishment verdict is issued. As long as bad faith set up attempts succeed they will continue to be used.

### Indicators of Bad Faith Set Up

Some of the more common red flags of a bad faith set-up include the following:

1. The claimant makes a policy limits settlement demand quickly after an accident, thereby depriving the insurer of the ability to conduct a full investigation. Such quick demands are combined with a limited amount of time to accept, again, in the hopes that records cannot be obtained and the investigation cannot be completed within that limited time period, and the settlement will be refused.

2. The claimant making a settlement offer with one or more unusual acceptance conditions.

3. The involvement of the claimant's counsel pre-dates certain medical or psychiatric care (e.g., testing and treatment for alleged mild traumatic brain injury).

4. The claimant seeks treatment from doctors with whom the claimant's counsel has a pre-existing relationship.

5. The level of pain or disability reported "post-lawyer involvement" is greater than indicated by the medical records existing "pre- lawyer involvement".

6. Adequate proof of lost income is not forthcoming.

7. Where there are multiple plaintiffs in a single accident and the all retain the same lawyer and are treated by the same chiropractor or physician.

8. Multiple plaintiffs in a low impact auto accident all claiming similar injuries.

9. The correspondence from the claimant's counsel is peppered with self-serving rhetoric, designed to impress the jury – and establish themes – for use in the bad faith follow-on lawsuit.

## Manufactured Litigation

Some courts recognize "set-up" or manufactured bad faith situations where claimants make settlement demands with unrealistic time limitations or otherwise force the insurance company to make a settlement decision without full access to information bearing on liability and damages. Where the court recognizes these factors, the insurance company may not be liable for failure to accept the settlement because the excess judgment or settlement was not due to the insurance company's "unreasonable" conduct but was driven by the motives of the plaintiff. [*Wade v. Emcasco Ins. Co.*, 483 F.3d 657 (10th Cir. 2007)]

Plaintiffs' delay in providing promised medical records and manipulation of settlement deadlines was for the purpose of setting up a bad faith claim was found in Glenn *v. Fleming,* 799 P.2d 79 (Kan. 1990) and *Miel v. State Farm Mutual Auto. Ins. Co.*, 912 P.2d 1333, 1339 (Ariz. App. 1995).

The emergence of the bad faith set-up has not gone unnoticed by the courts. One of the lead opinions articulating concerns with the conduct of claimant's counsel in the context of the set-up case is *Wade v. Emcaso Ins. Co.*, 483 F.3d 657 (10th Cir. 2007) (applying Kansas law). After reviewing some of the central historical decisions, the Tenth Circuit summarized its concern over what it referred to as "manufactured" litigation as follows:

In light of these decisions, we agree with the district court's observation that courts should exercise caution 'when the gravamen of the complaint is not that the insurer has *refused* a settlement offer, but that it has *delayed* in accepting one.' Mem. Op. 14 (citing *Adduci*, 53 Ill. Dec. 854, 424 N.E.2d at 649; *Pavia v. State Farm Mut. Auto. Ins Co.*, 82 N.Y.2d 445, 605 N.Y.S.2d 208, 626 N.E.2d 24, 28-29 (1993)). This caution 'arises from the desire to avoid creating the incentive to manufacture bad faith claims by shortening the length of the settlement offer, while starving the insurer of the information needed to make a fair appraisal of the case.' *Id.* at 15. As the First Circuit commented in *Peckham v. Continental Casualty Insurance Co.*, 895 F.2d 830, 835 (1st Cir. 1990): [T]he doctrinal impetus for insurance bad faith claims derives from the idea that the insured must be treated fairly and his legitimate interests protected.

Courts should exercise caution when the gravamen of the complaint is not that the insurer has refused a settlement offer, but that it has delayed in accepting one. This caution arises from the desire to avoid creating the incentive to manufacture bad faith claims by shortening the length of the settlement offer, while starving the insurer of the information needed to make a fair appraisal of the case. [*Wade v. Emcasco Ins. Co.*, 483 F.3d 657 (10th Cir., 2007)]

The doctrinal impetus for insurance bad faith claims derives from the idea that the insured must be treated fairly and his legitimate interests protected. The justification for bad faith jurisprudence is as a shield for insureds. The tort of bad faith should not, although it often is, be used as a sword for claimants. Courts should not permit bad faith in the insurance milieu to become a game of cat-and-mouse between claimants and insurer, letting claimants induce damages that they then seek to recover, while relegating the insured to the sidelines as if only a mildly curious spectator.

Permitting an injured plaintiff's chosen timetable for settlement to govern the bad-faith inquiry would promote the customary manufacturing of bad-faith claims, especially in cases where an insured of meager means is covered by a policy of insurance which could finance only a fraction of the damages in a serious personal injury case. Insurers would be bombarded with settlement offers imposing arbitrary deadlines and would be encouraged to prematurely settle their insureds' claims at the earliest possible opportunity in contravention of their contractual right and obligation of thorough investigation.

The cause of action for failure to settle is meant to protect the interests of the insured by requiring the insurer to conduct the litigation, including settlement negotiations, as if the insurance contract had no policy limits. It is not meant to create an artificial incentive for third-party claimants to reject otherwise reasonable settlement offers that are within the policy limits. A court should never turn the cause of action on its head by holding an insurance company liable where it eventually offered to settle the claim for the policy limits only to find that the claimant/plaintiff rejected the offer precisely in order to manufacture a lawsuit against the insurer for bad-faith refusal to settle.

For example, in *DeLaune v. Liberty Mut. Ins. Co.*, 314 So. 2d 601 (Fla. 4th DCA. 1975), plaintiffs made an offer to settle their claim stemming from an automobile accident for the $10,000 policy limit, attaching a 10-day deadline for the defense to accept the offer. Defense counsel, believing that settlement for the policy limits was possible, but not yet authorized to approve the settlement, contacted the plaintiffs' counsel on the last day of the deadline and asked for an extension of the offer until the following Monday after the Friday deadline. The plaintiffs refused and initiated a common law bad faith action for the excess judgment.

In affirming the judgment in the insurer's favor on the bad faith claim, the Fourth District recognized the plaintiffs' attempt to set up a bad faith claim, and stated:

"[T]he evidence fails to prove any negligence, much less negligence rising to the level of bad faith. The accident happened December 27, 1971. In less than a month suit was filed. Defense counsel received the file to defend eleven days later. Eight days after that plaintiffs' counsel offered to settle for the policy limits but limited the time for acceptance to ten days. It is the latter aspect of the offer which we find totally unreasonable under these circumstances. In view of the short space of time between the accident and the institution of suit, the provision of the offer to settle limiting acceptance to ten days made it virtually impossible to make an intelligent acceptance. Nor does the enclosure of an affidavit from a doctor stating that the injured plaintiff would be totally disabled warrant a different conclusion. Since when does one party to a lawsuit have to accept at face value the medical information furnished by the other party without even any inquiry? The evidence here shows that appellee, its adjusters, and its counsel proceeded with all due haste to determine and evaluate their position, and they almost made plaintiffs' unreasonable deadline. It should be noted that the personal injury case went to trial ten months after the deadline, so the time limitation was not invoked because the trial was imminent. Finally, to demonstrate that this whole charade might have been a "set up" for just such a suit as we are considering (as argued by appellee) when Monday came, after the Friday deadline, and the home office authorized settlement, plaintiffs' counsel refused it."

When there is no good faith reason why a settlement must be accomplished by a unilaterally set deadline, rather than mere days later, there should be, as the DeLaune court recognized, no claim for bad faith based on the insurer's acceptance shortly after the specified deadline. Instead, the insurer's efforts to settle should bar such a claim.

The Massachusetts Court of Appeals affirmed an award of over $1 million on a policy with limits of $20,000/$40,000 in *Gore v. Arbella Mutual Insurance Co.* 932 N.E.2d 837 (Mass. App. Ct. 2010). Holding that the trial court was entitled to award multiple damages on a $450,000 consent judgment entered against the insured under the Massachusetts claims handling statute the appeals court remanded for the trial court to decide whether to award double or treble damages on the consent judgment. The trial court doubled the consent judgment, based on its conclusion that Arbella's conduct was willfully reckless but "probably not malicious." [*Dattilo v. Arbella Mut. Ins. Co.*, No. 20024510, 2010 WL 4071754, at *1 (Mass. Super. Ct. Sept. 3, 2010), review denied, 458 Mass. 1111 (2010).]

The *Gore* dispute arose out of an accident that occurred when Anthony Caban struck a car driven by Angelina Dattilo. Arbella insured Caban under a policy with liability limits of $20,000 per person and $40,000 per accident. Shortly after the accident, Dattilo's attorney sent Arbella a letter detailing Caban's liability and Dattilo's injuries, enclosing medical records totaling over $25,000, and demanding that Arbella tender the $20,000-per-person policy limits within 30 days. The demand letter offered to fully release Caban and Arbella in exchange for the $20,000 limit.

Rejecting Arbella's contention that the plaintiff's demand letter constituted an attempt to "manufacture a bad faith insurance claim," the appeals court held that the plaintiff's alleged tactics, even if established, would not "as a matter of law, relieve Arbella of its duty to respond to a demand when liability was clear and damages exceeded the policy limits." The court reaffirmed that a "claimant's conduct is not relevant to the insurer's duty" to attempt to effectuate a settlement when liability and damages are reasonably clear.

An insured/claimant who retracts or rejects a settlement offer based on arbitrary deadlines or mere technicalities may have objectives other than settlement on his or her mind and may not be acting in good faith to try to reach a settlement. The insured's effort to create a bad faith claim may thwart the settlement of claims that otherwise could have been settled. When that occurs, the insured is forced into an adversarial relationship with the insurer. There also may be additional litigation that could have been avoided.

Bad faith claims have been manufactured as noted in *Berges v. Infinity Ins. Co.,* 896 So.2d 665, 686 (Fla.2004) (Wells, J., dissenting) where the court noted that it should recognize that it has the responsibility to reserve bad faith damages, which is limitless, court-created insurance, to egregious circumstances of delay and bad faith acts. The Court likewise has a responsibility to not allow contrived bad faith claims that are the product of sophisticated legal strategies and not the product of actual bad faith. [*United Auto. Ins. Co. v. Estate of Levine,* 87 So.3d 782, 788 (Fla. 3d DCA 2011); and *Safeway Ins. Co., Inc. v. Guerrero,* 83 P.3d 560, 207 Ariz. 82 (Ariz. App., 2004)]

In *Kemp v. Hudgins*, 133 F.Supp.3d 1271 (D. Kan., 2015) the District Court concluded that the uncontroverted evidence establishes that Kemp rejected each policy limit settlement proposal after the lawsuit was filed because he did not believe that the policy limits sufficiently covered his claim. The fee agreement with plaintiff's counsel provided that Copeland would only be paid if he recovered more than the policy limits on behalf of Kemp. And Kemp's multi-million-dollar stipulated judgment offer made clear that Kemp was not interested in settling the claim for the policy limit. While Kemp's circumstances changed in terms of his litigation expenses after January 2010, he would not have incurred attorneys' fees had he accepted Dairyland's March or

July policy limit offers. Kemp never offered a policy limits settlement after January 2010, and Dairyland repeatedly offered to settle for its policy limit. Kemp's settlement proposals establish that even if Dairyland accepted his offers, an excess judgment would have been entered in this case and Kemp would have pursued a bad faith claim against Dairyland to recover that amount.

Bad faith cases that are manufactured to avoid a settlement expand the concept of "bad faith" beyond what the case law and statutes require for "good faith." Ultimately, bad faith claims have become so common that the stringent standard actually needed to prove the tort of bad faith appears to have been ignored and bad faith claims allowed based on mere technical failures in reaching a settlement. Mistakes, negligence, and miscues do not meet the standard required for a bad faith claim. Rather, the insurer must have wrongfully refused to settle the claim when it should have done so if it had been acting fairly and honestly toward the insured. Submitting settlement payment a few days after an arbitrary deadline and disagreeing over the specific release language contained in a settlement proposal may be negligent, but that does not satisfy the high standard of deliberately wrongful conduct that should be required to support a bad faith action.

As a result of the absence of any clearly defined statutory guidelines for determining bad faith, the tactics used to set up bad faith claims are actually distorting the meaning of the bad faith statutes and case law and are slowly whittling away at its purpose altogether.

Although there undoubtedly may be situations in which an insurer engages in bad faith in the handling of claims, the duty of good faith should be precisely and carefully defined, so that only legitimate bad faith conduct results in bad faith judgments. A bad faith claim only should exist for egregious conduct, and state legislatures should create and define exact guidelines and limitations to these actions. The Fair Claims Settlement Practices statutes and Regulations attempt to do so but a close review of the Regulations indicate a clear bias in favor of policyholders and against insurers so that any apparent violation of the statutes or regulations is sufficient to allow a policyholder to establish a bad faith suit with ease.

The obligation to seek to settle insurance claims in good faith should be a two-way street. Parties should not be trying to evade an insurer's efforts to settle in order to expand policy limits. The claim for "bad faith" failure to settle should be exactly that — only for situations in which the insurer truly is refusing in bad faith to settle, not when it is in fact attempting to settle the claim. The statutory scheme has been abused in many instances and should be amended to balance the scales and ensure it carries out the intended purpose of achieving settlements of disputed insurance claims.

Courts should recognize that they have the responsibility to reserve bad faith damages, which is limitless, court-created insurance, to egregious circumstances of delay and bad faith acts. The Court likewise has a responsibility to not allow contrived bad faith claims that are the product of sophisticated legal strategies and not the product of actual bad faith.

Understanding how disruptive and costly it can be to defend against a bad faith lawsuit, prudent insurers strive to adhere to a range of best practices to lessen their exposure to, and strengthen their defenses against, bad faith claims.

To avoid the bad faith set up and avoid overzealous plaintiffs' counsel from causing a bad faith suit insurers must:

- Maintain ongoing training to help claim examiners spot and respond to "red flags" that evidence efforts to establish bad faith claims;
- Create specialized teams to handle potential bad faith claims;
- Carefully supervise claims staff to ensure that claims are handled in a timely and professional manner;
- Split files between defense and coverage matters and between multiple insureds or claimants in appropriate circumstances;
- Closely monitor claims in "problem" jurisdictions where bad faith suits bring about insupportable gigantic punitive damages claims against insurers.

## The Great Jewel Theft

*The stories that follows is based on fact. The names, places and descriptions have been changed to protect the guilty. This story was written for the purpose of providing insurers, those in the insurance business, and the insurance buying public sufficient information to recognize and join in the fight against insurance fraud.*

The Insured purchased, for the first time in his life, a policy of Personal Articles Floater Insurance (PAF) scheduling $125,000 worth of ladies' jewelry. When he first acquired the insurance, he advised the insurer that the jewelry was always kept in a class E safe (one that requires at least 30 minutes to drill out the lock) at his residence. He also told the insurer that he was employed full time as the owner of a gasoline service station and that he had never been canceled or suffered a previous loss.

One month after the policy was issued, just before the first installment of the premium finance contract was due, the Insured reported a loss. He claimed that two armed robbers came to his door at midnight (while his wife and child were fortuitously away helping a neighbor fill out immigration and naturalization forms) and forced him, at gun point, to open the safe. They removed only the jewels, struck him on the head with the weapon, and tied him up like a mummy with 56 feet of rope they just happened to have the foresight to bring with them.

On investigation, it was learned that the Insured had owned the jewelry for over twenty years. The Insured received the jewelry as a gift from his grandmother when he immigrated to the United States. The Insured came from what was then known as Soviet Armenia with his entire family of six. His jewels had been stored in his closet without incident for the full twenty years. Neither the Insured's father nor any of his relatives knew about the gift because "it was not their business to know."

The Insured, also because it was not his business to know, did not know whether his father or his brothers had received a similar gift from his grandmother. The Insured had resided in an apartment building owned by his father for many years, but just two months before buying insurance, he had moved into this new residence. Shortly after the robbery, he moved back to the family owned apartment house.

In truth, the Insured did not own a service station and was, in fact, unemployed for two years before the robbery. His father owned a service station and the Insured would sometimes, for no pay, help his father. Further, just before the policy was issued, his residence was burglarized of jewelry not scheduled on the PAF, but he claimed he "forgot" to tell the insurer about it.

The Insured had once owned a service station. He lost his franchise when the franchiser found out he was running multiple credit card slips from customers and forging their signatures on the slips. He eventually pleaded guilty to a forgery charge and was placed on probation.

The jeweler who appraised the jewelry stated to the insurance adjuster that he could replace it all for 50% of the appraised value. Investigation revealed that the Insured had suffered multiple losses of automobiles (the same car was stolen three times in two years) and he earned large sums from automobile accidents.

The Insured and his entire extended family were always together in the car and went to the same chiropractor for treatment whenever an accident happened. The Insured and the family used the same lawyer to represent their interest against the insurers for the parties who they claimed caused the accidents.

The Insurer denied the claim for the loss of the jewelry because the insured obtained the policy by means of misrepresentation of material fact and concealment of material fact. The Insured sued it for breach of contract and breach of the covenant of good faith and fair dealing seeking both compensatory and punitive damages The Court was reluctant to strike them, although evidence was ample that the insurer had good cause to reject the claim.

Discovery in the lawsuit established that the Insured and his father had reported the identical diamond ring stolen one year apart and had made the mistake of having it appraised by the same jeweler. The jeweler was willing to testify to the identity of the stones. Discovery also established two warranty violations in the policy.

Such facts were sufficient to establish fraud. However, when the defendant is an insurer, fraud is not that easy to establish. The litigation dragged on for four and one-half years; the trial court would not grant summary judgment. The Judge wished to give the Insured his "day in court" to prove that he was but an innocent dupe of the insurer. The case was set for trial and the Insured/Plaintiff made an offer of settlement that he would release the insurer of all liability in exchange for $30,000.00 cash.

By this time, with interest at 10% per annum, building over time, the exposure was at least $200,000.00 in compensatory damages and the possibility of excessive amounts in punitive damages if the jury disagreed with the position of the insurer. Counsel for the insurer was obligated to point out to his client that the cost, in attorneys' fees and expert witness fees, needed to take the matter through a trial by jury would probably exceed the $30,000.00 demand, not to mention the cost to resolve any necessary post-trial motions and appeals.

Although advised of the fraudulent claim police and prosecutors were not interested. The Insured had nothing to lose since he never owned the jewelry in the first place and concluded that $30,000 recovery – even after paying a contingent fee to his lawyer -- was better than a judgment giving him nothing.

To the insurer the exposure was too big and the potential gain was too small. The insurer, convinced that the Insured had perpetrated a fraud, especially after he made an offer to settle for less than 15% of the amount of the insurance, paid. It was happy, in fact, to be rid of the exposure.

Members of the public, and the insurance industry as a whole, lost as a result of this economic judgment. The same Insured has presented, at least, four apparently fraudulent claims. His father also collected for the theft of the identical ring and they enjoyed the proceeds of their fraud.

If insurance fraud is to be stopped, the profit must be taken out of it. Since prosecutors seem disinterested, it is necessary for the insurance industry to take the chance on a punitive damage award and try every case where they believe fraud is being perpetrated. If they continue to take the easy, and least expensive way out, the cost to the industry as a whole will multiply. Of course, insurers have shareholders who want to make a profit on their investment. Taking chances like those I propose will gain the ire of the shareholders and that is why this jewel theft claim – although nothing was owed – was a logical and prudent decision.

Prosecutors must be educated that insurance fraud is a serious crime that is taking multiple billions of dollars from the insurance industry. The cost of fraud is too big to continually pass on to the honest insurance consumer. If the prosecutors had taken note of the reports they received from the insurer the insureds would have been arrested and convicted and the insured's law suit would have been immediately dismissed.

Perhaps if fraud did not make insurance so expensive the number of honest consumers would be larger. Now, it appears to be a very small group. An insurance research group has found that more than 67% of all auto insurance claims in Los Angeles are fraudulent to some degree.

Twenty years later the insured was arrested, tried and convicted of being the leader of a terrorist and criminal organization called the Armenian Mafia. He is now serving a long term in federal penitentiary.

## Life Insurance Can Be Hazardous to Your Health

The Hungarian owned and operated a board and care facility for the aging in Carson City, Nevada. He brought his younger brother over from Hungary in 1975 to help him in the business. It was only a twenty-bed facility and with little help, the two could manage the entire business.

The oldest brother was the thinker. He got an honorary Ph.D. from the New World Society of Abundant Consciousness that ran a school in the desert just north of Pahrump. After receiving his honorary degree for a donation of $15,000, he insisted on the title doctor.

The doctor had no training in any field. He had a high school diploma and had operated several restaurants before buying the board and care facility. He believed that the title conferred on him the right to prescribe medicine, to give psychological advice, and to do anything he pleased. He would get drugs for his patients from other than legitimate sources. He would bill their insurers as if they were prescription drugs prescribed by a staff physician.

His younger brother maintained the facility, cooked the meals for the residents, doubled as a nurse and ran the business. The doctor acted like royalty.

Since the small business required both to work if it was to make a profit, the business began to deteriorate. Cash flow was minimal. Patient services became almost nonexistent. The doctor skimmed as much money into his pocket as he could and keep the patients alive. Neither he nor his brother drew anything much than subsistence monies from the business.

The dedicated younger brother made the business work. He began to cut personal corners. First, he decided to drop a $100,000 life insurance policy. With the reduced earnings of the business, he could not afford to pay the premium.

The doctor, who used the same insurance agent, was told of the intent of the brother to cancel. The doctor asked the agent to keep the policy in effect without his brother's knowledge. The doctor would pay the premium as a business expense of the board and care facility.

The agent, not wishing to lose his commission, agreed and kept in the policy in force, accepting premium payments from the doctor.

The younger brother suffered from severe hypertension. His controlled the disease by diet and medications. He trusted his older brother. He thought his older brother was wise and knowledgeable. He thought his older brother had, at least, the same level of expertise as any physician and trusted his brother more than a physician.

After the doctor had paid the first monthly premium on the life insurance policy, he explained to his brother that the hypertension drugs prescribed for him were dangerous. He told his younger brother that he had in the inventory of the board and care facility drugs that were more effective. Since they were in the stock of the facility the doctor could give them to his brother at no cost. The brother stopped taking his prescribed medicine and started taking the drugs given him by his brother. The doctor did not tell his brother that the drugs contained digitalis. Digitalis is a drug that, although useful in reducing chest pains in people with heart conditions, is poisonous in the amounts the doctor told his brother to take. It is even more poisonous to a person with hypertension.

Within two weeks of taking his brother's drugs, the younger brother was found by his wife apparently dead, on his kitchen floor. Paramedics arrived and immediately began CPR. Because she did not know what to do after calling the paramedics, the wife called her brother-in-law. He arrived at the scene about the same time as the paramedics. He was hysterical and interfered with the paramedics. They had to forcibly remove him from his brother so they could perform CPR. They put the brother in an ambulance and began racing toward the emergency hospital with red lights and siren. The doctor followed and almost sideswiped the ambulance twice. They called for police help on their radio. A Carson City police officer pulled the doctor off to the side of the road and restrained him for sufficient time to allow the ambulance to arrive at the hospital.

They could not revive the younger brother. They pronounced him dead one hour after arrival at the hospital. The doctor convinced the wife there should be no autopsy. His brother, her husband, had a severe heart condition that was well documented. He explained that there should be no reason to cut his body to satisfy a local ordinance. The doctor convinced the brother's family physician to sign the death certificate showing the cause of death as a heart attack. The family physician did so without evidence of such a heart attack. The family physician had not even seen the deceased within six months of his death. The family physician clearly violated the law. He thought the death certificate would help the family who appeared adamantly against the invasive procedures of an autopsy.

The widow was not an intelligent woman. She had limited education in her country of birth, Hungary. She could barely read or write the English language and spoke it with a thick accent. She relied totally on her brother-in-law. He handled the disposition of her husband's estate. She signed whatever papers he put before her.

One paper he put in front of her was a claim form making claim on the life insurance policy. The claim form did not use the sister-in-law's address but, rather, a P.O. box held in secret by the doctor. The insurance company, presented with an appropriate claim form signed by the widow and what appeared to be a proper death certificate, immediately issued its check for $100,000 plus interest, made payable to the widow, the sole beneficiary named in the policy.

The doctor received the check. He signed the widow's name to it and deposited the money in his account. He used the money to pay the debts of the board and care facility and to buy a new home for himself of five acres of desert property outside Carson City. The widow was left with nothing but debts. She sold the home. After paying a commission to the realtor and the funeral expenses she had only $1,000 left. Her brother-in-law loaned her $10,000 which she used to buy some secondhand furniture and move into a small apartment. She met a blackjack dealer at a casino and married him so she would have some means of support.

The doctor lived in luxury for a year off the proceeds and then began planning his next insurance fraud. He has no other brothers to kill, so he decided to obtain life insurance on the residents of the board and care facility.

Adapted from Barry Zalma's Kindle book and Paperback book, "Heads I Win, Tails You Lose" available as a Kindle Book and available as a Kindle Book.

## Negligent Supervision Does Not Eliminate Auto Use Exclusion

### Crashing an ATV on Public Roads Not a Homeowners Policy Loss

Lawyers are creative. They take a clear and unambiguous policy exclusion, accept it, and then claim it doesn't apply because there is another non-excluded cause of the injury. The Court of Appeal of Oregon acknowledged the creativity, ignored it, and, as it should, applied the clear and unambiguous language of the policy.

In *Brodi Epps, By And Through His Guardian Ad Litem, Molly S. Epps v. Farmers Insurance Exchange*, an inter-insurance exchange, et al., and Truck Insurance Exchange, an inter-insurance exchange, dba Farmers Insurance Company of Oregon; John Douglas Pollard; and Alta Lorena Hise-Pollard, 295 Or App 385, No. 604 A166532, Court of Appeals of the State of Oregon (December 12, 2018) the plaintiff sought coverage for the negligent entrustment of a minor to a drunk who took the minor on an off premises all terrain vehicle (ATV) ride.

### FACTS

Plaintiff, by and through his guardian ad litem, began this declaratory judgment action to determine whether a homeowners' insurance policy that defendant had issued covers the liability of the insureds, the Pollards, in an underlying action against them. The trial court granted defendant's motion for summary judgment, ruling that the policy does not cover the Pollards' potential liability because of the motor vehicle exclusion in the policy.

Defendant sold a homeowners' insurance policy to John and Alta Pollard, which, subject to various exclusions, covered their personal liability for bodily injury to others. While the policy was in force, plaintiff's mother took plaintiff, who was just under two years old, to the Pollards' home and left plaintiff in Alta's care while plaintiff's mother ran errands. Alta knew that John was intoxicated but still allowed John to place plaintiff between his knees on an all-terrain vehicle (ATV) and drive around the premises without plaintiff wearing a helmet or protective gear. At some point, John drove the ATV onto a public road and ran the ATV into a fence, which caused the ATV to roll and eject plaintiff, causing plaintiff serious bodily injury.

The Pollards tendered an insurance claim to defendant, which defendant denied on the basis of the motor vehicle exclusion to coverage in the policy. Plaintiff then sued seeking declaratory judgment against defendant to determine whether the Pollards' homeowners' insurance policy covers the Pollards' liability in plaintiff's action against them.

As noted above, on appeal, plaintiff does not dispute the trial court's determination that his claim against John Pollard is excluded from coverage under the policy because the plaintiff's injuries resulted from the use of a motor vehicle off of the insured premises. Plaintiff argued that the trial court erred when it determined that the policy excluded coverage for Alta's negligence. The plaintiff believed that Alta's negligent supervision of plaintiff occurred on the insured premises and resulted in a foreseeable harm to plaintiff.

## ANALYSIS

In disputes such as this one, that turn on the meaning of an insurance policy, the primary and governing rule is to ascertain the intention of the parties and, to do so, the court must examine the terms and conditions of the policy, and where a particular term is not defined in the contract, by identifying that term's plain meaning. If the term is ambiguous, the court is required to examine that term within the context of the policy as a whole. If two or more plausible interpretations still remain, the court construes the term against the drafter and in favor of the insured.

The policy sets forth certain exclusions like "We do not cover bodily injury, property damage or personal injury which: ***** 7. results from the ownership, maintenance, use, loading or unloading of: ***** b. motor vehicles." The policy defines "motor vehicle" as "any *** motorized land vehicle designed for recreational use off public roads," but that definition does not include "a motorized land vehicle, not subject to motor vehicle registration, used only on an insured location."

Reading the exclusion and definition together, the apparent purpose of the exclusion is to require the insured to obtain separate liability insurance for recreational vehicles, except when they are "used only on an insured location." Once the ATV left the Pollards' property and was traveling on the public road, the ATV was a "motor vehicle" within the policy's definition.

Plaintiff, relying on the definition of "occurrence" in the policy, contends that Alta's negligent supervision of plaintiff on the insured premises "constituted an occurrence under the policy because [it] exposed the child to conditions resulting in bodily injury" and, because "the policy insures against" the use of the ATV on the insured premises, the policy coverage should extend to Alta's acts.

Plaintiff's construction of the policy ignores the applicability of the motor vehicle exclusion to occurrences that cause bodily injury. The policy unambiguously excludes coverage for "occurrences" which result in bodily injury, when the bodily injury "results from the *** use *** of" "motor vehicles" off the premises of the insured.

In this case, plaintiff's injuries were the result of John's and plaintiff's "use" of a "motor vehicle" on a public road. The policy specifically and unambiguously excludes coverage for bodily injury that results from the "use" of "motor vehicles," such as the one used in this case, and the application of the exclusion under the policy does not depend on plaintiff's theory of liability or the defendant against whom his claim is stated.

Plaintiff's negligent supervision claim is based on Alta's act of allowing plaintiff to use the ATV with John. The court of appeal concluded that this is not a case where there is an independent non-motor vehicle related cause of plaintiff's bodily injuries that would take the claim outside of the motor vehicle exclusion. John's and plaintiff's use of the ATV off the premises of the insured triggered the Pollards' alleged liability for plaintiff's bodily injuries, and the policy unambiguously excludes coverage for bodily injuries that result from such a use.

Because plaintiff's bodily injuries resulted from the use of the ATV off the premises of the insured, plaintiff's claim squarely falls within the exclusion for coverage, regardless of who the plaintiff sues or under what theory of liability plaintiff seeks to recover.

## ZALMA OPINION

There is no question that Alta was negligent when she let John take the child on an ATV ride. That negligence, however, did not cause the injury. The child was injured when John, drunk, ran the ATV into a tree and the child was ejected and incurred serious injury, a cause clearly and unambiguously excluded. The Pollards needed available auto insurance coverage for the incident rather than try to make a homeowners policy into an auto liability policy.

## The Pot Called the Kettle Black

*Insured Suspected of Fraud Unsuccessfully Charges Insurer with Fraud*

Often, people whose claim was correctly rejected will attempt to obtain coverage by claiming that the insurer defrauded the person insured. In *Terry Granger v. The Travelers Home And Marine Insurance Co.,* No. 04-17-00814-CV, Fourth Court of Appeals San Antonio, Texas (December 12, 2018) Terry Granger appealed a summary judgment dismissing her breach of contract and common law fraud causes of action against The Travelers Home and Marine Insurance Company.

### BACKGROUND

Granger purchased a Renter's Insurance Policy from Travelers (the Policy). The Policy provided coverage against personal property loss caused by theft. The Policy included the standard conditions for the insured's duties, the requirement to testify at examination under oath (EUO) and to submit a sworn proof of loss. In addition the policy contained a private limitation of action provision prohibiting suit against the insurer unless there has been full compliance with all of the terms under Section I of this policy and suit is brought against the insurer within two years and one day after the cause of action accrues.

While the Policy was in force, Granger submitted a claim for coverage for the loss of personal property from an alleged burglary of her rental residence. After Granger's claim was made, Travelers notified Granger she was required to complete a proof of loss, provide documentation of the stolen property, and submit to an examination under oath. Granger failed to respond to Travelers's requests. Travelers sent Granger a letter closing her claim. Granger later filed her lawsuit against Travelers alleging breach of contract.

Travelers filed a motion for summary judgment as a matter of law alleging that Granger's breach of contract claims were barred by the Policy's "two years and one day" limitations condition. Subsequently, Granger amended her petition to include a common law fraud claim by which she claimed that her landlord, who she alleges was also an agent for Travelers, falsely represented to her that the limitations period for filing any insurance claim was four years. The trial court granted Travelers's motion for summary judgment on both claims.

## BREACH OF CONTRACT CLAIM

In her first issue, Granger argues that the Policy's "two-years-and-one-day" limit is not supported by consideration. Granger contends that the uncontroverted summary judgment evidence shows she did not receive consideration for her relinquishment of the four-year limitations period defined in section 16.051. Accordingly, Granger insists, the two-years-and-one-day limitation does not apply to her and her lawsuit against Travelers is not barred.

Generally, the limitations period for a breach of contract cause of action is four years after the day the cause of action accrues. However, parties to a transaction may agree to the time in which a person must file suit on a given cause of action.

The appellate court concluded that the policy's limitation provision of two years and one day to file a cause of action against Travelers is valid and binding.

The Policy's language is unambiguous. The premium Granger paid was consideration for all provisions contained in the Policy, including the two-years-and-one-day limitation provision. Accordingly, Granger's argument that additional consideration for the reduction in the limitations period was necessary failed as a matter of law.

Because Granger filed her suit more than two years and one day after Travelers denied her claim, Granger's cause of action for breach of contract is, as a matter of law, barred by the Policy's limitation period.

## COMMON LAW FRAUD

A common law fraud claim requires a material misrepresentation, which was false, and which was either known to be false when made or was asserted without knowledge of its truth, which was intended to be acted upon, which was relied upon, and which caused injury.

Granger submitted no evidence that Travelers assigned Detweiler (Granger's landlord) to present the Policy to Granger or to explain its conditions, especially the limitations condition, to her. There is no evidence that Travelers controlled Detweiler's tasks. There is likewise no evidence that Travelers permitted Detweiler to hold himself as an agent with authority to explain the limitations portion of the Policy or that it knowingly or voluntarily permitted Detweiler to misstate the limitations period to file a claim against Travelers. Granger failed to meet her burden to present some evidence that established that Detweiler had apparent authority to act for Travelers. The appellate court concluded that Travelers's no-evidence motion for summary judgment on the common law fraud was properly granted because there was no evidence that any alleged fraud on Detweiler's part can be imputed to Travelers under the theory of apparent authority.

## ZALMA OPINION

It would seem that the reason that Granger waited more than two years after her claim was denied was a desire to not appear for an EUO and that Travelers suspected fraud. Then, with utmost and unmitigated gall she claimed she was defrauded because her landlord – who had no agency relationship with Travelers and did not appear on the policy as the agent – told her the four year state statute of limitations applied and the private limitation of action provision did not apply. The claims were grasps in the dark and failed.

## Duty to Defend Only Applies to Person Sued

### No Right to Rescind a Contract that Does Not Exist

Liability insurance is designed to provide defense and indemnity to persons insured who are sued as a result of events covered by the insurance policy. It does not, nor can it, provide defense to a person not insured. Further, a liability policy will not defend if a clear and unambiguous exclusion applies.

In *Robert Mau; Eagle Well Services, Inc. v. Twin City Fire Insurance Co.*, No. 17-3392, United States Court of Appeals For the Eighth Circuit (December 6, 2018) Robert Mau and Eagle Well Services, Inc. ("EWS") failed in its efforts to get defense and indemnity from Twin City. They then appealed the district court's grant of Twin City Fire Insurance Company's ("Twin City") cross-motion for summary judgment.

### THE AVAILABLE COVERAGE

Twin City insured Eagle Operating, Inc. and its subsidiaries. Endorsement No. 2 of the policy defined Eagle Operating's subsidiaries to include EWS and MW Industries, Inc. During the relevant period, Mau was president of Eagle Operating, shareholder and president of EWS, director and president of MW, and an owner of American Well Services ("AWS").

In February 2012, EWS sold its assets to a predecessor of Sun Well Services ("Sun Well") through an Asset Purchase Agreement ("Agreement"). EWS and Mau were parties to the Agreement, which included a noncompetition covenant.

### BREACH OF A NONCOMPETITION CONTRACT

After the Agreement was signed, MW sold equipment to AWS. Claiming that the sale violated the noncompetition covenant, Sun Well sued Mau for breach of contract, fraud, and civil conspiracy, and it sued EWS for breach of contract and fraud. Twin City refused to defend the suit.

## THE DECLARATORY RELIEF ACTION

Mau and EWS sued Twin City, seeking a declaration that they were insured under the policy. They also sued Twin City for breach of contract and breach of the implied covenant of good faith and fair dealing. Mau filed a motion for partial summary judgment. Twin City filed a response in opposition and a cross-motion for summary judgment, asking the court to find that Twin City had no duty to defend Mau or EWS. The district court denied Mau's motion for partial summary judgment, and it granted Twin City's cross-motion for summary judgment.

North Dakota law applies in this case. An insurer has no duty to defend an action if there is no possibility of coverage under the policy. Any doubt about whether a duty to defend exists must be resolved in favor of the insured.

Mau argued before the district court that Twin City owed him a duty to defend because Sun Well sued him in his capacity as a director and officer of MW, an insured subsidiary of Eagle Operating. The district court rejected his argument. Sun Well's claims do not depend on any actions Mau took as president of MW. This is evidenced by the fact that Sun Well did not sue MW. While Sun Well's complaint mentions MW contextually, MW is not a party to the suit. There is no need for an insurer to defend a party who was not sued.

Instead, Sun Well's claims depend on the alleged breach of the noncompetition covenant in the Agreement between EWS and Sun Well, an agreement to which MW was not a party. Sun Well would have no claim for breach of contract, fraud, or civil conspiracy against Mau were it not for the Agreement, which he signed as president of EWS, not as a director and officer of MW. Thus, Sun Well sued Mau in his capacity as president of EWS. Because Sun Well's complaint contains no claims based on any actions Mau took as a director and officer of MW, Twin City owes him no duty to defend on that basis.

Eagle Operating's insurance policy with Twin City includes an exclusion that applies to Mau in his capacity as president of EWS. The dual service exclusion provides as follows: "The Insurer shall not pay Loss: . . . of an Insured Person based upon, arising from, or in any way related to such Insured Person's service, at any time, as a director, officer, trustee, regent, governor or equivalent executive or as an employee of any entity other than an Insured Entity even if such service is at the direction or request of such Insured Entity...."

Because the allegations of the complaint govern the duty to defend, the appellate court looks to Sun Well's complaint when applying the dual service exclusion. The complaint says that Mau "participated in the formation and subsequent operation" of AWS. And it says that AWS is an "affiliate" of Mau "as that term is defined in Section 7.13 of the [Agreement]." Any loss Mau suffers from the Sun Well litigation certainly "arises from" and is "related to" his service in one of the exclusion's stipulated roles for AWS, an uninsured entity. Thus, the dual service exclusion applies to Mau.

Because Mau was not sued in his capacity as director and officer of MW and because the dual service exclusion applies, there is no possibility of coverage for Mau under Twin City's policy.

Similarly, Twin City has no duty to defend EWS in this suit. The insurance policy includes another exclusion that reads as follows: "The Insurer shall not pay Loss under Insuring Agreement (C) in connection with any Claim based upon, arising from, or in any way related to any actual or alleged: ¶ (1) liability under any contract or agreement, provided that this exclusion shall not apply to the extent that liability would have been incurred in the absence of such contract or agreement . . . ."

In other words, the contract exclusion applies to claims arising from the insured's contracts or agreements unless liability otherwise would exist in the absence of the contract or agreement. This exclusion applies to EWS because Sun Well's claims against EWS for breach of contract and fraud are based upon, arise from, or are related to the Agreement, and liability could not have been incurred in the absence of the Agreement.

EWS does not contest that Sun Well's claims are based upon, arise from, or are related to the Agreement. EWS argues that Sun Well's fraud claim created the possibility that the Agreement would be rescinded. If the Agreement were to be rescinded, EWS claims, liability would exist in the absence of the Agreement.

In either case, even if EWS's arguments had some validity, the contract exclusion would apply to any resulting liability. Sun Well's fraud claim would not exist in the absence of the Agreement. The fraud claim alleged that Mau and EWS "concealed" material facts about their plan to breach the noncompetition covenant that they had a duty to disclose. And a contract that does not exist cannot be rescinded.

There is no possibility of coverage for EWS under Twin City's policy because the contract exclusion applies.

Applying North Dakota law, the court held that Twin City owed no duty to defend Mau in his capacity as director and officer of MW because no claims were brought against him in that capacity and, in any event, the dual service exclusion applied. The court also held that Twin City did not owe a duty to defend EWS where the claims against it for breach of contract and fraud are based upon the Asset Purchase Agreement and liability could not have been incurred in absence of the Agreement. Furthermore, even if EWS's arguments had some validity, the contract exclusion would apply to any resulting liability.

## ZALMA OPINION

Liability insurance is not designed to protect against breaches of contracts which, by definition, must be neither contingent nor unknown losses and are, therefore, not insurable. Breaching a non-competition clause is, by definition, an intentional act. Since fortuity is required for coverage under a liability policy an intentional breach of contract can never be the subject of insurance. Finally, there can never be an obligation of an insurer to do the impossible – defend an insured who was not sued.

## The Author

Barry Zalma is an insurance coverage consultant and Certified Fraud Examiner who now limits his practice to consultation, arbitration or mediation of insurance disputes. He is the founder of Barry Zalma, Inc., a California law firm whose practice emphasized the representation of insurers and those in the business of insurance.

Mr. Zalma is the author of many books, e-books, continuing education courses, and articles relating to insurance coverage, insurance claims handling and insurance litigation. His books and e-books on Insurance Claims, Construction Defects, Mold and Insurance Law are available ClaimSchool, Inc., The American Bar Association, Thompson Reuters, and Fastcase.com's Full Court Press. Details available at

He is an internationally recognized expert on insurance claims handling, insurance coverage, insurance fraud investigations, the commercial general liability policy, the comprehensive general liability policy, the homeowners policy, all first and third party insurance policies, inland marine coverages, and the tort of bad faith at http://zalma.com/blog/insurance-claims-library/

www.ingramcontent.com/pod-product-compliance
Lightning Source LLC
Chambersburg PA
CBHW071310220526
45468CB00001B/320